Beginning App Development with Flutter

Create Cross-Platform Mobile Apps

Rap Payne

Apress®

Beginning App Development with Flutter: Create Cross-Platform Mobile Apps

Rap Payne
Dallas, TX, USA

ISBN-13 (pbk): 978-1-4842-5180-5   ISBN-13 (electronic): 978-1-4842-5181-2
https://doi.org/10.1007/978-1-4842-5181-2

Managing Director, Apress Media LLC: Welmoed Spahr
Acquisitions Editor: Aaron Black
Development Editor: James Markham
Coordinating Editor: Jessica Vakili

Distributed to the book trade worldwide by Springer Science+Business Media New York, 233 Spring Street, 6th Floor, New York, NY 10013. Phone 1-800-SPRINGER, fax (201) 348-4505, e-mail orders-ny@springer-sbm.com, or visit www.springeronline.com. Apress Media, LLC is a California LLC and the sole member (owner) is Springer Science + Business Media Finance Inc (SSBM Finance Inc). SSBM Finance Inc is a **Delaware** corporation.

For information on translations, please e-mail rights@apress.com, or visit http://www.apress.com/rights-permissions.

Apress titles may be purchased in bulk for academic, corporate, or promotional use. eBook versions and licenses are also available for most titles. For more information, reference our Print and eBook Bulk Sales web page at http://www.apress.com/bulk-sales.

Any source code or other supplementary material referenced by the author in this book is available to readers on GitHub via the book's product page, located at www.apress.com/978-1-4842-5180-5. For more detailed information, please visit http://www.apress.com/source-code.

Printed on acid-free paper

This book is dedicated to the men and women of the Flutter Community. I've never seen a group more devoted to the success of others. You're an inspiration and example to me.

Particular thanks to these members of the community who've helped me with Flutter issues. This Texan owes y'all!

Andrew "Red" Brogdon (Columbus, Ohio),

Brian Egan (Montana),

Emily Fortuna (San Francisco),

Frederik Schwieger (Düsseldorf, Germany), Jeroen "Jay" Meijer (Rotterdam, Netherlands), Martin Rybak (New York), Martin Jeret (Estonia), Nash Ramdial (Trinidad), Nilay Yenner (San Francisco), Norbert Kozsir (Karlsruhe, Germany), Pooja Bhaumik (Bengaluru, India), Raouf Rahiche (Casablanca by way of Algeria), Remi Rousselet (Paris), Rohan Tanaja (Berlin), Scott Stoll (Cleveland, Ohio),

But especially Simon Lightfoot (London), who we all call "The Flutter Whisperer" He taught me much of what I know about Flutter.

Praise for Beginning App Development with Flutter

"Rap has written a great starting guide full of information for those who are new to developing multi-platform apps with Flutter."

—Frederik Schwieger (Düsseldorf, Germany), Organizer of the
International Flutter Hackathon and creator of flutter school

"A great read! This covers everything a beginner might want to know, and more. It explains not only what Flutter is but why it exists works the way it does. It also provides great tips for common pitfalls along the way. Definitely recommended."

—Jeroen "Jay" Meijer (Rotterdam, Netherlands),
Leader of Flutter Community Github

"Rap's book is a great book to get started with Flutter. It covers every important topic to write your very first app but also contains valuable information for more seasoned developers."

—Norbert Kozsir (Karlsruhe, Germany)
Flutter Community Editor

"As a non-native English speaker, I'm totally impressed by the simplicity of this book and how much I can read and understand without getting bored."

—Raouf Rahiche (Algeria) Flutter speaker,
developer, and instructor

"As an early adopter and one of the original members of the Flutter Community, Rap is one of the world's foremost authorities on Flutter. Where documentation is written for Engineers, by Engineers, Rap is a human who (thankfully!) writes in an enjoyable style that can easily be understood by other humans."

—Scott Stoll (Cleveland, Ohio), Contributor to the Flutter codebase and Co-founder of the Flutter Study Group

Table of Contents

About the Author

 **Rap Payne** has focused on mobile development since he started Agile Gadgets, a mobile app development company, in 2003. He is a consultant, trainer, and entrepreneur who has written apps, mentored developers, and taught software development classes for Fortune 500 companies like Boeing, Walmart, Coca-Cola, Wells Fargo, Honda, CVS, GE, Chase, HP, Lockheed, ExxonMobil, Lowe's, Nike, J.C. Penney, USAA, and Walgreens; government agencies like the NSA, the US Air Force, Navy, Army, NASA, Britain's GCHQ, and Canada's postal service; and several provincial governments, to name a few.

As a professional mentor and trainer, Rap has developed a talent for communicating highly complex ideas in easy-to-understand ways. And as a real-world developer, he understands the need to teach these topics using practical and realistic examples and exercises.

About the Technical Reviewer

 **Massimo Nardone** has more than 22 years of experience in Security, Web/Mobile development, Cloud, and IT Architecture. His true IT passions are Security and Android.

He has been programming and teaching how to program with Android, Perl, PHP, Java, VB, Python, C/C++, and MySQL for more than 20 years.

He holds a Master of Science in Computing Science from the University of Salerno, Italy.

He has worked as a Project Manager, Software Engineer, Research Engineer, Chief Security Architect, Information Security Manager, PCI/SCADA Auditor, and Senior Lead IT Security/Cloud/SCADA Architect for many years.

His technical skills include Security, Android, Cloud, Java, MySQL, Drupal, Cobol, Perl, Web/Mobile development, MongoDB, D3, Joomla, Couchbase, C/C++, WebGL, Python, Pro Rails, django CMS, Jekyll, Scratch, and so on.

He works as Chief Information Security Officer (CISO) for Cargotec Oyj.

He worked as visiting lecturer and supervisor for exercises at the Networking Laboratory of the Helsinki University of Technology (Aalto University). He holds four international patents (PKI, SIP, SAML, and Proxy areas).

Who is this book for?

If you're a developer with experience in some object-oriented language like Java, C#, C++, or Objective-C and you want to create Android apps, iOS apps, or web apps with Flutter, this book is for you. It is especially important for you if you want to create an app that runs on multiple platforms and if you are new to Flutter.

If you've got some experience already with Flutter, you'll undoubtedly learn something, but we're not expecting that you have any prerequisite knowledge or experience with Flutter. All of our chapters are written with the assumption that everything in Flutter is completely new to you.

If you know anything about iOS development, Android development, or web development, that will certainly help with understanding the topics because there are lots of analogies in them for Flutter. The more you know about those things, the better, especially JavaScript and React. But if you know none of them, don't fret. They're by no means necessary.

Knowledge of the Dart language also will help. We've found that Dart has got its unique features for sure, but it is extremely easy to pick up if you understand object-oriented concepts. Heck, if you know Java or C#, most code snippets are understandable without any explanation of the language. Read a few and you'll be writing your own in no time.

At the same time, there are some unique but very cool Dart features that we consider best practices. We could have "simplified" the code for Java devs by not using these best practices, but in the long run that's not doing you any favors. Instead, we go ahead and use them, but we do explain those things in "Appendix A: Dart Language Overview." In there, we give you a cheat sheet with just enough detail to write code, followed by a more in-depth explanation of the features that will be unexpected by developers of other languages. Pay special attention to the section called "Unexpected things about Dart."

What is covered?

This book teaches you how to create fully functioning and feature-rich apps that run on iOS, Android, and the Web. We do this in three sections.

Part I: Introduction to Flutter

1. **Hello Flutter** – We're setting the stage for the book. Giving you a feel for why you're here. What problems does Flutter solve? Why the boss would choose Flutter vs. some other solution.

2. **Developing in Flutter** – Flutter has a unique set of tools, but it isn't always straightforward what each tool does and how to use it. This chapter guides you through the process of write-debug-test-run. We get an understanding of the tooling including installation and maintenance.

Part II: Foundational Flutter

3. **Everything Is Widgets** – Widgets are super important to Flutter since they're the building blocks of every Flutter app. We show why and provide the motivation and basic tools to create widgets. Topics include composition, UI as code, widget types, keys, and stateless vs. stateful widgets.

4. **Value Widgets** – A deep dive into widgets that hold a value, especially user-input fields. Topics include the pubspec.yaml file; Text, Image, and Icon widgets; and how to create forms in Flutter.

5. **Responding to Gestures** – How to make your program do things in response to user actions like taps, swiping, pinching, and the like. We'll show you the button family and the GestureDetector widget.

6. **Laying Out Your Widgets** – We'll learn how to lay out a view, controlling how widgets are placed side by side and/or above and below, defining the amount of space between widgets, and aligning them vertically and horizontally.

7. **Navigation and Routing** – Navigation is making the app hide one widget and show another in response to user actions. This makes them feel like they're moving from one scene to another. We'll cover stack navigation, tab navigation, and drawer navigation.

8. **Styling Your Widgets** – Then we'll look at how to control each widget's color, borders, decorations, shapes, and other presentational characteristics. We handled light styling as we introduced each widget earlier, but this is where we answer all the questions needed to get a real-world app looking good and staying consistent throughout with themes.

9. **Managing State** – How to get data from one widget to another and how to change that data. We cover how to create StatefulWidgets and design them in the best way. We also provide a high-level overview of tools to handle real-world complex state management.

Part III: Above and Beyond

10. **Your Flutter App Can Work with Files** – Using libraries. Futures, async, await. Bundling files with your app. Reading and writing a file. JSON serialization.

11. **Making RESTful API Calls with Ajax** – How to read from and write to an HTTP API server. This is where we show how to make GET, POST, PUT, DELETE, and PATCH requests.

12. **Using Firebase with Flutter** – We will show you a real-world, robust cloud solution that works like a dream with Flutter. No surprise that it is also a Google offering.

What is not covered and where can I find it?

As importantly, you should know what not to expect in the book. We will not give you a primer on the Dart programming language beyond the aforementioned appendix. We simply didn't think it was the best use of your time and wanted to dive right into Flutter. If you feel you need a primer later on, go here: `https://dart.dev/guides/language/language-tour` followed by `https://dart.dev/tutorials`. We chose not to discuss deploying to the app stores. The stores already do a fine job of explaining how to submit an app. That, and the process, changes so frequently that your definitive resource ought to be the stores themselves. You'll find instructions at `https://developer.apple.com/ios/submit/` and here: `https://play.google.com/apps/publish`. And we aren't going to cover certain advanced topics like device-specific development in iOS and Android or adding Flutter to an existing iOS/Android project. This is a beginner's book and we didn't want to overwhelm you. These and so many other topics can be found on the Web by searching and through some of the other resources we'll point you to in the last chapter of book.

PART I

Introduction to Flutter

CHAPTER 1

Hello Flutter

Picture this in your mind's eye. You are the superintelligent and capable CEO of a new business. Obviously your mission is to maximize sales while minimizing expenses. "Hmmm.", you think. "I can really increase sales if I make our products available on the Web." So you ask your friends how to create a web app and they say …

"You need to hire a web developer. They should know HTML, CSS, JavaScript, and probably some framework like React, Vue, or Angular."

It's expensive but you do it and your gamble pays off. Sales increase markedly. Trying to keep on top of demand, you monitor social media and engage your customers. You hear them say that this web app is great and all but "We'd have been here earlier if you had an app in the App Store." So you talk to your team who, while being experts in the Web, are not iOS developers. They tell you …

"You need to hire an iOS expert. They should know iOS, Swift or Objective-C, Xcode, macOS, and CocoaPods for development."

Your research shows that this person is <u>even more</u> specialized and therefore expensive than your web devs. But again, it seems to be the right thing to do, so you bite the bullet and hire them. But even while this app is being developed, you see that the feedback was not isolated to iOS apps, but instead was looking at all mobile devices. And – oh, snap! – 85% of devices worldwide run Android, not iOS. You bury your head in your hands as you ponder whether or not you can afford to ignore 85% of your potential customers. Your advisors tell you …

© Rap Payne 2019
R. Payne, *Beginning App Development with Flutter*,
https://doi.org/10.1007/978-1-4842-5181-2_1

"You need to hire an Android expert. They should know the Android OS, Gradle, Android SDK, XML, Android Studio, and Java or Kotlin."

"Really?!? Another developer?", you say. "Yes. And one just as expensive as your iOS developer," they respond.

Isn't there one person who can do all three things? Some way to share the code between all of those environments? Then you could hire just one person. In fact, they could write the code one time and deploy it to the Web, to the App Store, and to the Google Play Store. One codebase to maintain. One place to make improvements and upgrades. One place to squash bugs.

Ladies and gentlemen, allow me to introduce you to Flutter!

What is Flutter?

Flutter is a set of tooling that allows us to create beautiful apps that run on iOS, Android, the Web, and desktop.[1]

Flutter is ...

- Free (as in free beer. No cost)

- Open source (that's the other sense of the word "free")

- Backed by and originated at Google

- Being enhanced and maintained by a team of developers at Google and hundreds of non-Google contributors around the globe

- Currently being used by thousands of developers in organizations across the world for production apps

- Fast because it compiles to truly native apps that don't use crutches like WebViews and JavaScript bridges

---

[1]Desktop is coming soon. Flutter will work on Windows, macOS, Chromebooks, and Linux.

- Written one place and compiled to a web app for billions of browsers, an iOS app for iPhones and iPads, and an Android app for all of the rest of the phones and tablets out there

Why Flutter?

Google's mission with Flutter is ...

To build a better way to develop for mobile

Notice what is <u>not</u> in that mission. There's no mention of Android (which is also owned by Google) nor of iOS nor of the Web. Flutter's goal is to create a better way to develop for all devices. In other words, Flutter should be better to create iOS apps than Swift. It should be better to create Android apps than Kotlin. It should be better to create web apps than HTML/JavaScript. And if you get all of those things simultaneously with one codebase, all the better.

The Flutter team has succeeded spectacularly with this mission.

As proof, Eric Seidel offers this example.[2] The Google CRM team used Flutter to build an internal Android app and did it **three times** faster than with their traditional Android toolchain!

But it turns out that Flutter isn't the only game in town for cross-platform. You have other options.

The other options

Cross-platform development comes in three general flavors listed in Table 1-1.

---

[2]http://bit.ly/eric_seidel_flutter_keynote_video at 21:47 in.

Table 1-1. *Cross-platform development categories*

	Some technologies	Cons	Pros
Progressive Web Apps (PWA)	HTML/CSS, React, Angular, Vue	Not a real app. Runs in a web browser. Not available in app stores. Hard to create a desktop shortcut. Cannot access many of the device's resources like accelerometer, compass, proximity sensor, Bluetooth, NFC, and more	Easy to write
Hybrid	PhoneGap, Cordova, Sencha, Ionic	Runs in a WebView so it can be slow. Nearly impossible to share code with the web app	Easier for web devs to learn because it uses HTML and JavaScript as its language and structure
Compile- to-native solutions	React Native, NativeScript, Flutter, Xamarin	Learning a framework may be difficult. Mastering the toolchain definitely is	Real apps that can be found in the stores and run fast

If you have a captive audience, one where users value your app so much that they're willing to accept a poorer user experience, the cheapest solution is to create a PWA. If your app is extremely naive and speed is not expected to be an issue, a hybrid solution might be appropriate. But if speed, smoothness, and sophisticated capability are important, you will need to go with a native solution.

Native solutions

As of today, there are four fairly popular compile-to-native solutions (Table 1-2).

Table 1-2. *Compile-to-native cross-platform frameworks*

	Xamarin	NativeScript	React Native	Flutter
Year introduced	2011	2014	2015	2018
Backed by	Microsoft	Telerik	Facebook	Google
Presentation language	XAML and/or xamarin.forms	Proprietary but looks like XML	Proprietary but looks like JSX	Dart
Procedural language	C#	JavaScript	JavaScript	Dart

These are all decent options. All are free to develop in and are well-tested, having many production applications created. All have been used in large organizations.

But only one has an option to create a web application in addition to the iOS and Android apps that will be deployed to the app stores – Flutter.

Flutter is the latest of these frameworks to be released. As such it has a distinct advantage of observing those that had come before. The Flutter team took note of what worked well with other frameworks and what failed. In addition, Flutter added new innovations and ideas – all baked in from the start rather than being bolted on as improvements are made.

But I suspect that if you've bought this book, you don't need much convincing so I'll stop. Suffice it to say that Flutter is amazing! It is easy to write, elegant, well-designed – an absolute pleasure to code in.[3]

Conclusion

Now, if you're the kind of developer I hope you are, you're chomping at the bit to get your hands dirty writing some code! So let's get to it. We'll start by installing and learning the Flutter development toolchain.

---

[3]But if you do want to read more, here's a deeper discussion of Flutter vs. some other frameworks: `http://bit.ly/2HC9Khm`

CHAPTER 2

Developing in Flutter

As we saw in the last chapter, Flutter enables us to create apps that run on the Web, on desktop computers, and on mobile devices (which seems to be the main draw). But wait a second, how exactly do we create these apps? What editor should we use? What is needed in the Flutter project? How do you compile the Dart source code? Do we need any other tools to support the project? How do you get it into a browser or on a device in order to test it out? Good questions, right?

Let's answer those questions and more in this chapter. Let's cover two significant topics:

1. Tools needed – How to install and maintain them

2. The development process – How to create the app, run it, and debug it

---

Caution   By its nature, cross-platform app development tooling involves an awful lot of moving parts from various organizations, few of whom consult with the others before making changes. And since we're dealing with boundary-pushing and young technology, changes happen frequently. We've tried in this chapter to stick with timeless information but even it is likely to become stale eventually. Please check with the authors of these tools for the latest and greatest information.

© Rap Payne 2019
R. Payne, *Beginning App Development with Flutter,*
https://doi.org/10.1007/978-1-4842-5181-2_2

The Flutter toolchain

There is no end to the list of helpful tools that the development community has produced. It is truly overwhelming. We're making no attempt at covering them all. We want to give you just enough for you to be proficient but not so many that you're overburdened. Forgive me if I've skipped your favorite.

The Flutter SDK

The Flutter SDK is the only indispensable tool. It includes the Flutter compiler, project creator, device manager, test runner, and tools that diagnose – and even correct – problems with the Flutter configuration.

Installing the flutter SDK

The installation instructions are found here: `https://flutter.dev/docs/ get-started/install`. Long story short – it will involve downloading the latest zip file of tools and setting your PATH to point to the folder where you unzipped them. The steps vary per operating system, but they're very plain on that web site.

Tip   This step seems very low level and sounds intimidating, but after this step, things get easier and less error-prone. Don't let it discourage you.

IDEs

In theory an IDE isn't really needed. Flutter can be written using any editor and then compiled and run using the flutter SDK that you installed earlier. But in reality almost nobody ever does that. Why would they? The following IDEs have Flutter support built right in!

VS Code from Microsoft

VS Code is from Microsoft. Its official name is "Microsoft Visual Studio Code," but most of us just call it *VS Code*. Whatever you call it, please do not confuse it with Microsoft's other product called "Microsoft Visual Studio." They are not the same thing regardless of the similar names.

You can get VS Code here: `https://code.visualstudio.com`.

Android Studio/IntelliJ from JetBrains

Android Studio and IntelliJ are essentially the same thing. They are built from the same codebase and have the same features.

You can get Android Studio at `https://developer.android.com/studio` and IntelliJ IDEA here: `www.jetbrains.com/idea/download`.

Which IDE should I use?

Both VS Code and Android Studio/IntelliJ are free and open source. Both run cross-platform on Windows, Mac, and Linux. Both are roughly equally popular with Flutter developers,[1] neither having a clear market advantage over the other. You can't go wrong with either one.

But if you must choose one, what we've found is that your background may affect how you like the tools. Developers from the web development world, those who use tech like HTML, CSS, JavaScript, NodeJS, React, Angular, or Vue, strongly prefer VS Code. On the other hand, those developers who came from a Java world, especially Android developers, seem to lean toward Android Studio/IntelliJ.

The good news is that this is a very low-pressure choice. It is trivial to switch editors – even while working on a given project. Start in one and see

---

[1]A recent poll of Flutter devs by Andrew Brogdon (@redbrogdon) of the Flutter team showed that 53% use VS Code, 30% use Android Studio, and 15% use IntelliJ. See `http://bit.ly/flutter_devtools_poll`

how you like it. If you don't, you can give the other a test drive for awhile. Go back and forth a couple of times until you have a strong preference. It's really no big deal to switch.

IDE DevTools

While those IDEs are great, they're not built for Flutter exclusively; they're used for developing in other languages and frameworks as well. So to improve the Flutter development flow, we should install the Flutter DevTools. It adds in debugger support, lets you look at logs, connects seamlessly with emulators, and a few more things.

Installing the DevTools is done from <u>within</u> each IDE. Within Android Studio/IntelliJ, go to "Preferences ➤ Plugins" from the main menu (Figure 2-1). In VS Code, go to "View ➤ Extensions" (Figure 2-2). The Flutter devtools are simply called "Flutter" and a search will turn them up. In either platform, hit the green "Install" button.

Figure 2-1. *DevTools install in Android Studio*

Figure 2-2. *DevTools install in VS Code*

You may need to restart the IDE after you install.

Emulators

Once you've got the IDE and DevTools installed, you're ready to compile your app. But to run it, you need to get it on a device. An emulator – a virtual device that runs on your laptop/desktop – makes it really easy to run, test, debug, and show your app. You'll probably want to test on both iOS and Android, so you'll need emulators for each. There are several emulators available, but I'll mention just a couple, Xcode's iOS simulator and AVD's Android emulator.

iOS simulator

If you don't own a Mac, you won't be running an iOS emulator or even compiling for iOS for that matter.[2] But if you do and you have Xcode installed, you're in luck; you have the iOS simulator already. To run it, you open Xcode, then go to Xcode ➤ Open Developer Tool ➤ Simulator (Figure 2-3). The simulator will start up, and from within it, you can select any iOS device including iPhones and iPads.

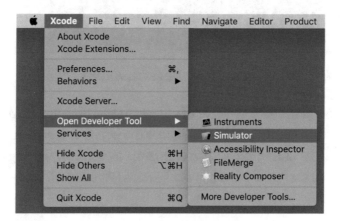

Figure 2-3. *Opening the iOS Simulator from Xcode*

---

[2]<sarcasm>Thanks, Apple.</sarcasm>

Android emulator

Just like there are tons of Android models, so are there tons of Android emulators, but there are only two popular ways to interact with them: Genymotion and AVD Manager. Genymotion is a for-profit company, so when you visit their web site, they'll do their level best to steer you toward their paid version. That's understandable. We'll focus on AVD Manager because it is totally free and more popular with Flutter devs.

AVD stands for "Android Virtual Device." The AVD Manager is found in Android Studio under Tools (Figure 2-4).

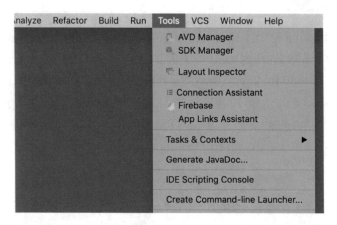

Figure 2-4. *Finding the AVD Manager in Android Studio*

Once opened, you'll see a list of your currently installed emulators. It should start out empty at first. You'll have the ability to install one or more of the hundreds of Android device emulators available by hitting the "+ Create Virtual Device..." button at the bottom (Figure 2-5).

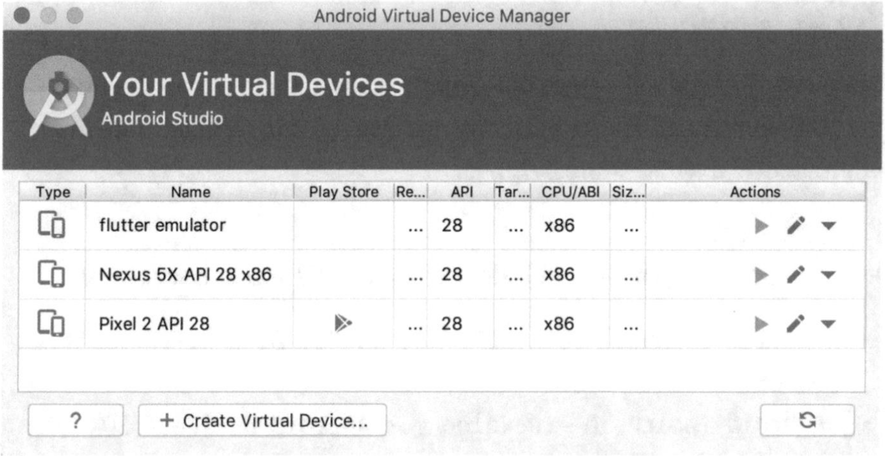

Figure 2-5. *AVD Manager has a list of available devices. Click "+" to add more*

Hit it and you can choose from all kinds of devices or create one of your own. You'll only need to install a device once. After it's installed, that emulated device is usable from any IDE, whether IntelliJ/Android Studio or VS Code. No need for a separate setup on VS Code.

Keeping the tools up to date

Early on, cross-platform development with tools like Xamarin and React Native was terribly difficult because of the sheer number of the tools involved and the interdependencies between them. I'm still in therapy from the pain.

But because Flutter arrived on the scene later it can learn from others' mistakes. The Flutter team, recognizing these pain points, gave us an innovative tool to manage the rest of the toolchain. It will examine your development machine, looking for all the tools you'll need to develop Flutter apps, the versions you have, the versions that are available, the interdependencies between them, and then make a diagnosis of problems. It will even prescribe a solution to those problems. Kind of sounds like a doctor, right? Well, let me introduce you to flutter doctor!

flutter doctor

You'll run flutter doctor from the command line. It checks all the tools in your toolchain and reports back any problems it encounters. Here's one where Xcode needed some help:

```
$ flutter doctor
Doctor summary (to see all details, run flutter doctor -v):

[✓] Flutter (Channel beta, vX.Y.Z, on Mac OS X X.Y.Z, locale
    en-US)
[✓] Android toolchain - develop for Android devices (SDK
    version X.Y.Z)
[!] Xcode - develop for iOS and macOS (Xcode X.Y)
    X Xcode requires additional components to be installed in
      order to run.
    Launch Xcode and install additional required components
    when prompted.
[✓] Android Studio (version X.Y)
[✓] VS Code (version X.Y.Z)
[!] Connected device
    ! No devices available

! Doctor found issues in 2 categories.
$
```

The "No devices available" error is common, and you can usually ignore that one. It just means that at that moment no emulators were running.

Here's an example of what we prefer to see – everything checks out:

```
$ flutter doctor
Doctor summary (to see all details, run flutter doctor -v):

[✓] Flutter (Channel beta, vX.Y.Z, on Mac OS X X.Y.Z, locale
    en-US)
```

[✓] Android toolchain - develop for Android devices (SDK
    version X.Y.Z)
[✓] Xcode - develop for iOS and macOS (Xcode X.Y)
[✓] Android Studio (version X.Y)
[✓] VS Code (version X.Y.Z)
[✓] Connected device (1 available)

• No issues found!

flutter doctor not only detects and reports problems but it usually prescribes the fix for each. It will even tell you when it is time to upgrade itself via "flutter upgrade."

flutter upgrade

Yes, the initial installation of the Flutter SDK was a little daunting but the upgrade is a breeze. You'll literally type two words, "flutter upgrade":

```
$ flutter upgrade
Upgrading Flutter from /usr/local/bin/flutter...
From https://github.com/flutter/flutter
   2d2a1ff..a72edc2  beta        -> origin/beta
   3932ffb..cc3ca9a  dev         -> origin/dev
   5a3a46a..a085635  master      -> origin/master
 * [new branch]      refactor    -> origin/refactor
<snip>
 * [new tag]         v1.10.5     -> v1.10.5
Updating c382b8e..a72edc2
 11 files changed, 413 insertions(+), 302 deletions(-)
Building flutter tool...

Upgrading engine...
Downloading ios-deploy...                           0.3s
```

```
Flutter X.Y.Z • channel beta • https://github.com/flutter/
flutter.git
Framework • revision a72e06 (23 hours ago) • 20XX-YY-ZZ
15:41:01 -0700
Engine • revision b863200c37
Tools • Dart X.Y.Z

Running flutter doctor...
Doctor summary (to see all details, run flutter doctor -v):
[✓] Flutter (Channel beta, vX.Y.Z, on Mac OS X X.Y.Z, locale
    en-US)
[✓] Android toolchain - develop for Android devices (SDK
    version X.Y.Z)
[✓] Xcode - develop for iOS and macOS (Xcode X.Y)
[✓] Android Studio (version X.Y)
[✓] VS Code (version X.Y.Z)
[✓] Connected device (1 available)

• No issues found!
```

Note that flutter doctor is automatically run as the last step, confirming that all is well. Upgrading is a piece of cake.

The Flutter development process

Now that we have all the tools installed and up to date, let's create an app and run it through the debugger.

Scaffolding the app and files

Create a whole new Flutter app by running ...

```
$ flutter create my_app
```

This will create a subfolder under the current folder called my_app. It will be full of ready-to-run Dart code.

Tip   The app name is case insensitive, so you should make it all lowercase. Dashes are illegal characters, so you can't use kebab-casing. The recommended casing is lowercase_with_underscores.

Anatomy of a Flutter project

It's not critical that you know about all of the files and folders that are in the project you just created. But if you're curious, let's quickly walk through a newly created Flutter project shown in Figure 2-6.

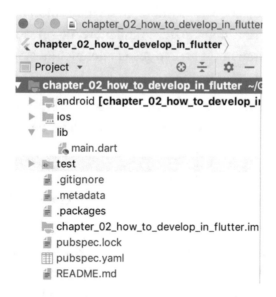

Figure 2-6. *A fresh Flutter project made by flutter create*

You'll have these folders:

- android and ios – These are the platform-specific parts of the project. For the most part, you won't need to touch these.

- lib – This is the home of all of your Dart source code. You will build your app's hierarchy here. This is where you'll spend nearly all of your time and attention.

- test – If you have unit tests (and you probably should eventually), put them here.

And you'll have these files:

- pubspec.yaml – This is essentially the project file for Dart projects. This is where we set our project name, description, dependencies and more. Be sure to read the comments in here to get a better picture of what is suggested and possible.

- .gitignore and README.md – These will be very familiar to devs who use git and github for their source code repository. Others won't care.

- .metadata and .packages – These are important config files which you'll never open. But Flutter needs them.

Tip   There's one more file you should be aware of: analysis-options. yaml. Having this file is not required, but if you do, you'll write better code. This file signals the IDE to perform linting (aka static analysis) on the code as you write it. With analysis-options.yaml, the IDE will warn you when you don't use best practices.

Rather than writing one from scratch, let me suggest that you start with someone else's. Here's one that is very popular with the Flutter

community: `https://github.com/flutter/plugins/blob/`
`master/analysis_options.yaml`.

It is aggressive. If you want to turn off some of the rules, just delete the lines or comment them out. An explanation of all of the linting rules can be found here: `http://dart-lang.github.io/`
`linter/lints/`.

Running your app

You now have a Flutter app created. Let's go run it. There are multiple ways of running your app. The most popular way is to hit the green "Play" button in either Android Studio/IntelliJ or VS Code. You can also do it from the command line using "flutter run":

```
$ flutter run
Running "flutter pub get" in chapter_02_how_to_develop_in_
flutter...                                            0.5s
Launching lib/main.dart on iPhone X in debug mode...
Running Xcode build...
 ├─Assembling Flutter resources...                    6.1s
 └─Compiling, linking and signing...                  5.9s
Xcode build done.                                     13.8s
Syncing files to device iPhone X...                1,852ms
```

To hot reload changes while running, press "r". To hot restart (and rebuild state), press "R".
```
An Observatory debugger and profiler on iPhone X is available
at: http://127.0.0.1:52550/8mOh8zacV58=/
For a more detailed help message, press "h". To detach, press
"d"; to quit, press "q".
```

But if you hit the green Play/Debug button in your IDE (Figure 2-7), you'll have the option of debugging your app by setting breakpoints and stepping through the code using the developer tools (Figure 2-8).

Figure 2-7. *The Play and Debug buttons are at the top in Android Studio*

Figure 2-8. *The Play button is in the upper left in VS Code*

Obviously you'll need to run your app in a device of some kind. There are several: the Chrome browser for a web app, emulators, or a physical device that is tethered to your development machine via a cable. When you click the Play/Debug button, you get to choose which device you want to run at that moment. Notice that in the preceding screenshot of Android Studio, there's a dropdown menu with a list of available devices. In VS Code, hit the Play button, and a menu immediately pops up with your choices. With either IDE, you are in control.

Tip   You can check what devices are currently available to you by running "flutter devices" from the command line.

```
$ flutter devices
3 connected devices:
```

```
Vivo XL3    • 55S...KF • android-arm64 • Android
8.0.0 (API 26)
Android SDK • emul...4 • android-x86   • Android 9
(API 28) (emulator)
iPhone X    • E6...39A • ios            • com.
apple...OS-12-1 (simulator)
```

The preceding sample output tells us that we have three devices. The first and second are Android devices and the third runs iOS. The first device is a tethered physical device. The second and third are emulators.

Note that this command is different from the "flutter emulators" command which tells you all possible emulators you could potentially choose from. The flutter devices command tells you which devices are currently available to run your app.

Running it as a web app

Flutter considers your browser to be a device when you're running as a web app. So all that is needed to run as a web app is to enable the Google Chrome web browser as a device. You can enable it with this one-time command:

```
$ flutter config --enable-web
Setting "enable-web" value to "true".
```

From then on, when you get a list of devices on which to run your app, "Chrome" will appear as one of them. Simply choose to run your app in Chrome and the IDE will load your web app in it.

Running it on a tethered device

There are times when you need to run your app on a physical device. For example, I was developing a project that involved printing labels to a physical printer connected by Bluetooth. Emulators don't pair via Bluetooth. To test the printing, I needed an actual physical device that was already paired to my Bluetooth printer.

To tether a physical device to your development machine, you'll use a USB cable for most Android devices and a Lightning cable for most iPhones.

Tips   #1 When connecting an Android device, it will initially think you're trying to charge it or transfer photos. To let it know you're trying to debug, open the Developer Options screen on the device and select "Enable USB debugging".

#2 Many connection issues can be caused by an inferior USB cable. Counterintuitively, not all USB cables are created equal. Switch to a higher-quality cable if you still can't connect after changing settings.

Hot reloading

Once the app is running in your emulator/browser/physical device/ whatever, you'll want to make changes to the source code and rerun. Here's the really cool thing: any time you save a change to the source code, it is recompiled and the new version is loaded instantly. Your app picks up where you left off – in the same spot, with the same state, and same data. We call it "hot reloading," and it makes the development cycle ridiculously fast and frictionless.

Debugging

Both IDEs have essentially the same debugging tools you've become accustomed to in all IDEs. When you start your project running, the debugging tools will appear.

In Android Studio the debug window opens, usually at the bottom of the IDE. It has a tiny toolbar which looks like Figure 2-9.

Figure 2-9. *The debugging toolbar in Android Studio*

The options are "step over," "step into," "force step into," and "step out" from left to right.

In VS Code the toolbar appears floating over your source code (Figure 2-10).

Figure 2-10. *The debugging toolbar in VS Code*

Its options are "play/pause," "step over," "step into," "step out," "hot reload," "restart," and "stop debugging."

Note   Flutter is pickier when you're debugging than when running for real in a device. This is a good thing because during debugging it makes obvious certain errors that you should probably fix but aren't necessarily fatal. In the release version, it swallows those same errors and (hopefully) allows our users to continue running our app.

One family of those errors is "runtime assertions." You'll know you're dealing with one of these when the debugger gives you an error like this:

```
══════════════ Exception caught by gesture ══════════════

The following assertion was thrown while handling a
gesture:
setState() callback argument returned a Future.
The setState() method on _FooState#236 was called
with a closure or method that returned a Future.
Maybe it is marked as "async".
etc. etc. etc.
```

Your takeaway is this: when you see one of these, fix the problem. It's the right thing to do. But don't be confused if you don't see that same problem after you've deployed it.

Conclusion

Look, I know that this is a lot of stuff to absorb. The nature of cross-platform development makes the tooling hairy. But the worst is behind us. Once you've got the Flutter SDK and an IDE (VS Code/Android Studio/IntelliJ IDEA) installed, that's all you really need. And granted, the DevTools and an emulator or two can really help. All that's left is getting some repetitions in for practice. You're going to be great!

So now that we've seen the Flutter toolchain, let's start creating widgets!

PART II

Foundational Flutter

CHAPTER 3

Everything Is Widgets

Let's pretend that you are an insanely talented Lego nerd and got offered one of the few coveted jobs as a Lego Master Builder. Congrats! Let's also say that your first assignment is to build a six-foot-tall Thor made from 26,000 Legos (Figure 3-1).

Figure 3-1. *A Lego Thor. The author snapped this picture at a movie theater once*

© Rap Payne 2019
R. Payne, *Beginning App Development with Flutter,*
https://doi.org/10.1007/978-1-4842-5181-2_3

How would you go about doing that? Ponder that for a minute. Go ahead, we'll wait.

Would you just start grabbing bricks and putting them together? Probably not. Would you lay out the soles of Thor's feet and build from the bottom up? Again, no. Here's my guess as to your common-sense strategy:

1. You'd get a vision of what you're building. Figure the whole thing out.

2. Realize that the entire project is too complex to build at once.

3. Break the project into sections (legs, left arm, right arm, torso, left sword, right sword, helmet, cape, head).

4. Realize that each of them is still too complex.

5. For each section, you break it into sub-sections.

6. Repeat steps 4 and 5 until you've got simple enough components that each is easy to understand, build, and maintain – for you and for any teammates that you may have.

7. Create each simple component.

8. Combine simple components to form the larger, more complex components.

9. Repeat steps 7 and 8 until you've got your entire project created.

This process has a name: *componentization,* and is exactly the thought process we'll go through with our Flutter projects.

Componentization is not something new. In fact, it was proposed as far back as 1968.[1] But the technique has recently exploded in popularity thanks to web frameworks like Angular, React, Vue, Polymer, and native web components. Seems like all the cool kids are doing software components these days. The idea of recursively breaking down the complex bits into simpler bits is called *decomposition*. And the act of putting the written pieces back together into larger components is called *composition*.

In the world of Flutter, these components are referred to as *widgets*. Flutter people like to say "everything is widgets," meaning that you and I will be using the Google-provided widgets – the ones that ship with Flutter. We'll compose them together to create our own custom widgets. And our custom widgets will be composed together to create more and more complex custom widgets. This continues until you've got yourself a full-blown app.

In the world of Flutter, components are referred to as **_widgets_***.*

Every app can be thought of in two parts:

1. Behavior – What the software <u>does</u>. All of the business logic goes here: the data reading, writing, and processing.

2. Presentation – How the software <u>looks</u>. The user interface. The buttons, textboxes, labels.

Only Flutter combines these into one language instead of two.

UI as code

Other development frameworks have proven componentization to be the way to go. The Flutter team has openly stated that they were heavily

---

[1]`http://bit.ly/componentHistory`

inspired by React[2] which is based on componentization. In fact, all framework makers seem to borrow heavily from one another. But Flutter is unique in the way that the user interface is expressed. Developers use the same Dart language to express an app's graphical user interface as well as the behavior (Table 3-1). We call this "UI as code."

Table 3-1. *Only Flutter uses the same language for presentation and behavior*

Framework	Behavior expressed in ...	UI expressed in ...
Xamarin	C#	XAML
React Native	JavaScript	JSX
NativeScript	JavaScript	XML
Flutter	Dart	Dart

So how does this UI get created? Like many other frameworks and languages, a flutter app starts with a *main* function. In Flutter, main will call a function called runApp(). This runApp() receives one widget, the root widget which can be named anything, but it should be a class that extends a Flutter StatelessWidget. It looks like this:

```
// import the Dart package needed for all Flutter apps
import 'package:flutter/material.dart';

// Here is main calling runApp
void main() => runApp(RootWidget());

// And here is your root widget
class RootWidget extends StatelessWidget {
  @override
```

---

[2]Source: https://flutter.dev/docs/resources/faq#does-flutter-come-with-a-framework

```
Widget build(BuildContext context) {
    return Text("Hello world");
  }
}
```

And that's all you need to create a "Hello world" in Flutter.

But wait … what is this Text() thing? It's a built-in Flutter widget. Since these built-in widgets are so important, we need to take a look at them.

Built-in Flutter widgets

Flutter's foundational widgets are the building blocks of everything we create and there are tons of them – about 160 at last count.[3] This is a lot of widgets for you and I to keep track. But if you mentally organize them, it becomes much more manageable.

They fall into these major categories:

- Value widgets

- Layout widgets

- Navigation widgets

- Other widgets

Note   These are not Flutter's official list of categories. Their 14 categories are listed here: `https://flutter.dev/docs/development/ui/widgets`. We just felt that reorganizing them helps to keep them straight.

---

[3]You can find a list of them all here: `https://flutter.dev/docs/reference/widgets`

We'll take a brief look at each of these categories with an example or two, and then we'll do some deep dives in later chapters. Let's start with value widgets.

Value widgets

Certain widgets hold a value, maybe values that came from local storage, a service on the Internet, or from the user themselves. These are used to display values to the user and to get values from the user into the app. The seminal example is the Text widget which displays a little bit of text. Another is the Image widget which displays a .jpg, .png, or another picture.

Here are some more value widgets:

Checkbox	FormField	RefreshIndicator
CircularProgressIndicator	Icon	RichText
Date & Time Pickers	IconButton	Slider
DataTable	Image	Switch
DropdownButton	LinearProgressIndicator	Text
FlatButton	PopupMenuButton	TextField
FloatingActionButton	Radio	Tooltip
FlutterLogo	RaisedButton	
Form	RawImage	

We'll explore value widgets in more detail in the next chapter.

Layout widgets

Layout widgets give us tons of control in making our scene lay out properly – placing widgets side by side or above and beneath, making them scrollable, making them wrap, determining the space around widgets so they don't feel crowded, and so on:

Align	FittedBox	Padding
AppBar	Flow	PageView
AspectRatio	FractionallySizedBox	Placeholder
Baseline	GridView	Row
BottomSheet	IndexedStack	Scaffold
ButtonBar	IntrinsicHeight	Scrollable
Card	IntrinsicWidth	Scrollbar
Center	LayoutBuilder	SingleChildScrollView
Column	LimitedBox	SizedBox
ConstrainedBox	ListBody	SizedOverflowBox
Container	ListTile	SliverAppBar
CustomMultiChildLayout	ListView	SnackBar
Divider	MediaQuery	Stack
Expanded	NestedScrollview	Table
ExpansionPanel	OverflowBox	Wrap

This is a huge topic which we've given its own chapter, Chapter 6, "Laying Out Your Widgets."

Navigation widgets

When your app has multiple scenes ("screens," "pages," whatever you want to call them), you'll need some way to move between them. That's where Navigation widgets come in. These will control how your user sees one scene and then moves to the next. Usually this is done when the user taps a button. And sometimes the navigation button is located on a tab bar or in a drawer that slides in from the left side of the screen. Here are some navigation widgets:

AlertDialog	MaterialApp	TabBar
BottomNavigationBar	Navigator	TabBarView
Drawer	SimpleDialog	

We'll learn how they work in Chapter 7, "Navigation and Routing."

Other widgets

And no, not all widgets fall into these neat categories. Let's lump the rest into a miscellaneous category. Here are some miscellaneous widgets:

GestureDetector	Cupertino	Transitions
Dismissible	Theme	Transforms

Many of these miscellaneous widgets are covered throughout the book where they fit naturally. GestureDetector is crucial enough that it gets its own chapter, Chapter 5, "Responding to Gestures."

How to create your own stateless widgets

So we know that we will be composing these built-in widgets to form our own custom widgets which will then be composed with other built-in widgets to eventually form an app.

Widgets are masterfully designed because each widget is easy to understand and therefore easy to maintain. Widgets are abstract from the outside while being logical and predictable on the inside. They are a dream to work with.

Every widget is a class that can have properties and methods. Every widget can have a constructor with zero or more parameters. And most importantly, every widget has a build method which receives a BuildContext[4] and returns a single Flutter widget. If you're ever wondering how a widget got to look the way it does, locate its build method:

---

[4]Don't get distracted by the BuildContext. It's used by the framework and we do occasionally refer to it, but we'll save those examples later in the book. For now, just think of it as part of the recipe to write a custom widget.

```
class RootWidget extends StatelessWidget {
  @override
  Widget build(BuildContext context) {
    return Text('Hello world');
  }
}
```

In this hello world example which we repeated from earlier in the chapter, we're displaying a Text widget (Figure 3-2). A single inner widget works but real-world apps will be a whole lot more complex. The root widget could be composed of many other subwidgets:

```
class FancyHelloWidget extends StatelessWidget {
  Widget build(BuildContext context) {
    return MaterialApp(
      home: Scaffold(
        appBar: AppBar(
          title: Text("A fancier app"),
        ),
        body: Container(
          alignment: Alignment.center,
          child: Text("Hello world"),
        ),
        floatingActionButton: FloatingActionButton(
          child: Icon(Icons.thumb_up),
          onPressed: () => {},
        ),
      ),
    );
  }
}
```

Figure 3-2. *The app created by this simple widget*

So as you can see, the build method is returning a single widget, a MaterialApp, but it contains a Scaffold which contains three subwidgets: an AppBar, a Container, and a FloatingActionButton (Figure 3-3). Each of those in turn contains sub-subwidgets of their own.

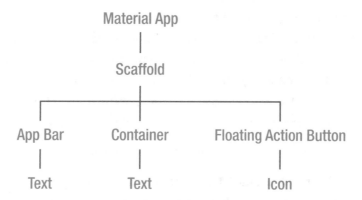

Figure 3-3. *The widget tree from our example app above*

This is how your build method will always work. It will return a single, massive, nested expression. It is widgets inside widgets inside widgets that enable you to create your own elaborate custom widget.

Widgets have keys

You may hear about a virtual DOM when other developers talk about Flutter. This comes from the world of React. (Remember that Flutter borrowed heavily from React's excellent architecture.) Well, strictly speaking, Flutter doesn't have a DOM, but it does maintain something resembling it – the element tree. The element tree is a tiny copy of all the widgets on the screen. Flutter maintains a current element tree and one with batched changes applied.

You see, Flutter might be really slow if it applied every tiny change to the screen and then tried to re-render it hundreds of times per second. Instead, Flutter applies all of those changes to a copy of the element tree. It then periodically "diffs" the current element tree with the modified one and decides what truly needs to be re-rendered. It only re-renders those parts that need it. This is much, much faster.

But occasionally Flutter gets confused when matching the widgets in the element trees. You'll know to programmatically assign keys if your data changes and widgets get drawn in the wrong location, the data isn't updated on the screen, or your scroll position isn't preserved.

You don't need to worry about keys most of the time. It is needed so rarely that we're going to be satisfied if you understand that ...

1. Keys exist and why Flutter may need them.

2. If your widgets aren't being redrawn as you might expect when data changes, keys may solve problems.

3. You have the opportunity to assign keys to certain widgets.

If that's not enough to satisfy you for now, the great Emily Fortuna has recorded a super ten-minute video on keys.[5]

Passing a value into your widget

Do you know what this formula means?

```
y = f(x)
```

Math majors will recognize this as reading "Y is a function of X." It concisely communicates that as X (the independent variable) changes, Y (the dependent variable) will change in a predictable way. Flutter lives on this idea, but in Flutter the formula reads like this:

```
Scene = f(Data)
```

In other words, as the data in your app changes, the screen will change accordingly. And you, the developer, get to decide how that data is presented as you write a build method in your widgets. It is a foundational concept of Flutter.

---

[5]You can find Emily's video here: `http://bit.ly/FlutterKeys`

Now how might that data change? There's two ways:

1. The widget can be re-rendered with new data passed from outside.

2. Data can be maintained <u>within</u> certain widgets.

Let's talk about the first. To pass data into a widget, you'll send it in as a constructor parameter like this:

```
Widget build(BuildContext context) {
  return Person("Sarah"); // Passing "Sarah" into a widget
}
```

If a widget represents how to render a Person, it would be a very normal thing to pass in a firstName, like we just did with "Sarah" earlier. If you do that, you'll need to write your widget's constructor to receive that value:

```
class Person extends StatelessWidget {
  final String firstName;
  Person(this.firstName) {}
  Widget build(BuildContext context) {
    return Text('$firstName');
  }
}
```

This is Dart syntax. Note three things. First, you'll list the input parameter in the constructor ("this.firstName" in the preceding example). Second, make sure you put "this." in front of it. The "this." matches it to a class-level property rather than a parameter that is local to the constructor function. And third, mark the corresponding class property as final.

You might want to pass in two or more properties like this:

```
Widget build(BuildContext context) {
  return Person("Sarah","Ali");
}
```

Of course passing in two values means creating two final variables and two constructor parameters to handle them:

```
class Person extends StatelessWidget {
  final String firstName;
  final String lastName;
  Person(this.firstName, this.lastName) {}
  Widget build(BuildContext context) {
    return Text('$firstName $lastName');
  }
}
```

As you can guess, these are matched positionally which can be easy to mess up and not terribly flexible. A better practice is to have named parameters:

```
Widget build(BuildContext context) {
  return Person(firstName:"Sarah", lastName:"Ali");
}
```

This reduces confusion for the other developers who use your widget. Here's how you'd write your widget to receive that value:

```
class Person extends StatelessWidget {
  final String firstName;
  final String lastName;
  Person({this.firstName, this.lastName}) {}
  Widget build(BuildContext context) {
    return Container(child: Text('$firstName $lastName'));
  }
}
```

Do you see the difference? It's subtle. There are now curly braces around the constructor parameters. This makes them optional and named.

Tip   Note that in all three of the preceding examples, we are using a Person class that might have been defined in the same dart file where you're using it. But a better practice is to create each class in a separate dart file and import it into other dart files where it is used.

```
import 'Person.dart';
```

Stateless and Stateful widgets

So far we've been going out of our way to create stateless widgets. So you probably guessed that there's also a stateful widget. You were right. A stateless widget is one that doesn't maintain its own state. A stateful widget does.

"State" in this context refers to data within the widget that can change during its lifetime. Think about our Person widget from earlier. If it's a widget that just displays the person's information, it should be stateless. But if it is a person **maintenance** widget where we allow the user to change the data by typing into a TextField, then we'd need a StatefulWidget.

There's a whole chapter on stateful widgets later. If you just can't wait to know more about them, you can read Chapter 9, "Managing State," later in this book. Then come back here.

So which one should I create?

The short answer is create a stateless widget. Never use a stateful widget until you must. Assume all widgets you make will be stateless and start them out that way. Refactor them into stateful widgets when you're sure you really do need state. But recognize that state can be avoided more often than developers think. Avoid it when you can to make widgets simpler and therefore easier to write, to maintain, and to extend. Your team members will thank you for it.

Note   There is actually a third type of widget, the InheritedWidget. You set a value in your InheritedWidget and any descendent can reach back up through the tree and ask for that data directly. It is kind of an advanced topic, but Rémi Rousselet would have had my head if I hadn't mentioned it. You can read more about it in Chapter 9, "Managing State," or watch Emily Fortuna's concise overview of InheritedWidget here: `http://bit.ly/inheritedWidget`.

Conclusion

So now we know that Flutter apps are all about widgets. You'll compose your own custom Stateless or Stateful widgets that have a build method which will render a tree of built-in Flutter widgets. So clearly we need to know about the built-in Flutter widgets which we'll learn beginning in the next chapter.

CHAPTER 4

Value Widgets

We learned in the last chapter that *everything is a widget.* Everything you create is a widget and everything that Flutter provides us is a widget. Sure, there are exceptions to that, but it never hurts to think of it this way, especially as you're getting started in Flutter. In this chapter we're going to drill down into the most fundamental group of widgets that Flutter provides us – the ones that hold a value. We'll talk about the Text widget, the Icon widget, and the Image widget, all of which display exactly what their names imply. Then we'll dive into the input widgets – ones designed to get input from the user.

The Text widget

If you want to display a string to the screen, the Text widget is what you'll need.

```
Text('Hello world'),
```

Tip If your Text is a literal, put the word const in front of it and the widget will be created at compile time instead of runtime. Your apk/ipa file will be slightly larger but they'll run faster on the device. Well worth it.

You have control over the Text's size, font, weight, color, and more with its style property. But we'll cover that in Chapter 8, "Styling Your Widgets."

© Rap Payne 2019
R. Payne, *Beginning App Development with Flutter,*
https://doi.org/10.1007/978-1-4842-5181-2_4

The Icon widget

Flutter comes with a rich set of built-in icons (Figure 4-1), from cameras to people to cards to vehicles to arrows to batteries to Android/iOS devices. A full list can be found here: `https://api.flutter.dev/flutter/material/Icons-class.html`.

Figure 4-1. *An assortment of Flutter's built-in widgets in random colors*

To place an icon, you use the Icon widget. No surprise there. You use the Icons class to specify which one. This class has hundreds of static values like Icons.phone_android and Icons.phone_iphone and Icons.cake. Each points to a different icon like the ones pictured previously. Here's how you'd put a big red birthday cake (Figure 4-2) on your app:

```
Icon(
  Icons.cake,
  color: Colors.red,
  size: 200,
)
```

Figure 4-2. *The red cake icon*

The Image widget

Displaying images in Flutter is a bit more complex than Text or Icons. It involves a few things:

1. Getting the image source – This could be an image embedded in the app itself or fetched live from the Internet. If the image will never change through the life of your app like a logo or decorations, it should be an embedded image.

2. Sizing it – Scaling it up or down to the right size and shape.

Embedded images

Embedded images are much faster but will increase your app's install size. To embed the image, put the image file in your project folder, probably in a subfolder called images just to keep things straight. Something like assets/ images will do nicely.

Then edit pubspec.yaml. Add this to it:

```
flutter:
  assets:
    - assets/images/photo1.png
    - assets/images/photo2.jpg
```

Save the file and run "flutter pub get" from the command line to have your project process the file.

Tip   The pubspec.yaml file holds all kinds of great information about your project. It holds project metadata like the name, description, repository location, and version number. It lists library dependencies and fonts. It is the go-to location for other developers new to your project. For any of you JavaScript developers, it is the package.json file of your Dart project.

Then you'll put the image in your custom widget by calling the asset() constructor like this:

```
Image.asset('assets/images/photo1.jpg',),
```

Network images

Network images are much more like what web developers might be accustomed to. It is simply fetching an image over the Internet via HTTP. You'll use the network constructor and pass in a URL as a string.

```
Image.network(imageUrl),
```

As you'd expect, these are slower than embedded images because there's a delay while the request is being sent to a server over the Internet and the image is being downloaded by your device. The advantage is that these images are live; any image can be loaded dynamically by simply changing the image URL.

Sizing an image

Images are nearly always put in a container. Not that this is a requirement, it's just that I can't imagine a real-world use case where it won't be inside another widget. The container has a say in the size that an image is drawn. It would be an amazing coincidence if the Image's natural size fit its container's size perfectly. Instead, Flutter's layout engine will shrink the image to fit its container, but not grow it. This fit is called *BoxFit. scaleDown,* and it makes sense for the default behavior. But what other options are available and how do we decide which to use? Table 4-1 provides your BoxFit options.

Table 4-1. *BoxFit options*

fill	Stretch it so that both the width and the height fit exactly. Distort the image	
cover	Shrink or grow until the space is filled. The top/bottom or sides will be clipped	
fitHeight	Make the height fit exactly. Clip the width or add extra space as needed	
fitWidth	Make the width fit. Clip the height or add extra space as needed	
contain	Shrink until both the height <u>and</u> the width fit. There will be extra space on the top/bottom or sides	

Photo courtesy of Eye for Ebony on Unsplash

So those are your options, but how do you choose? Figure 4-3 may help you decide which fit to use in different situations.

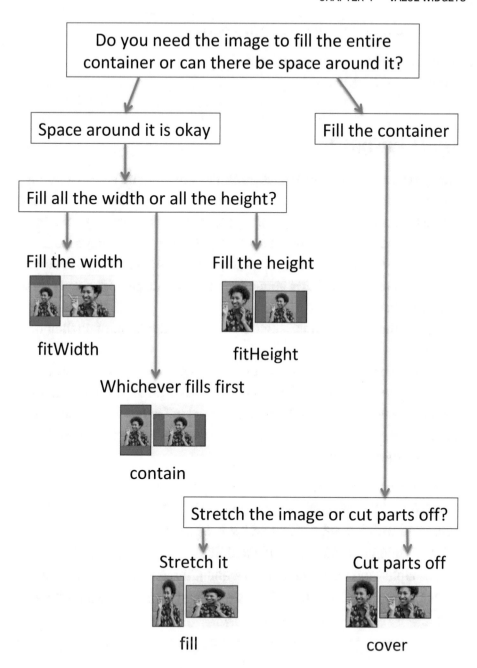

Figure 4-3. *How to decide an image's fit*

To specify the fit, you'll set the *fit* property.

```
Image.asset('assets/images/woman.jpg',
  fit: BoxFit.contain,),
```

Input widgets

Many of us came from a web background where from the very beginning there were HTML <form>s with <input>s and <select>s. All of these exist to enable the user to get data into web apps, an activity we can't live without in mobile apps as well. Flutter provides widgets for entering data like we have in the Web, but they don't work the same way. They take much more work to create and use. Sorry about that. But they are also safer and give us much more control.

Part of the complication is that these widgets don't maintain their own state; you have to do it manually.

Another part of the complication is that input widgets are unaware of each other. In other words, they don't play well together until you group them with a Form widget. We eventually need to focus on the Form widget. But before we do, let's study how to create text fields, checkboxes, radio buttons, sliders, and dropdowns.

Caution   Input widgets are really tough to work with unless they are used within a StatefulWidget because by nature, they change state. Remember that we mentioned StatefulWidgets briefly in the last chapter and we're going to talk about them in depth in Chapter 9, "Managing State." But until then, please just take our word for it and put them in a stateful widget for now.

Text fields

If all you have is a single textbox, you probably want a TextField widget. Here's a simple example of the TextField widget with a Text label above it:

```
const Text('Search terms'),
TextField(
  onChanged: (String val) => _searchTerm = val,
),
```

That onChanged property is an event handler that fires after every keystroke. It receives a single value – a String. This is the value that the user is typing. In the preceding example, we're setting a local variable called _searchTerm to whatever the user types.

To provide an initial value with a TextField, you need the unnecessarily complex TextInputController:

```
TextEditingController _controller =
    TextEditingController(text: "Initial value here");
```

Then tell your TextField about the controller

```
const Text('Search terms'),
TextField(
  controller: _controller,
  onChanged: (String val) => _searchTerm = val,
),
```

You can also use that _controller.text property to retrieve the value that the user is typing into the box.

Did you notice the Text('Search terms')? That is our lame attempt at putting a label above the TextField. There's a much, much better way. Check this out ...

Making your TextField fancy

There's a ton of options to make your TextField more useful – not infinite options, but lots. And they're all available through the InputDecoration widget (Figure 4-4):

```
return TextField(
  controller: _emailController,
  decoration: InputDecoration(
    labelText: 'Email',
    hintText: 'you@email.com',
    icon: Icon(Icons.contact_mail),
  ),
),
```

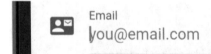

Figure 4-4. *A TextField with an InputDecoration*

Table 4-2 presents some more InputDecoration options.

Table 4-2. *Input decoration options*

Property	Description
labelText	Appears above the TextField. Tells the user what this TextField is for
hintText	Light ghost text inside the TextField. Disappears as the user begins typing
errorText	Error message that appears below the TextField. Usually in red. It is set automatically by validation (covered later), but you can set it manually if you need to

(continued)

Table 4-2. (*continued*)

Property	Description
prefixText	Text in the TextField to the left of the stuff the user types in
suffixText	Same as prefixText but to the far right
icon	Draws an icon to the left of the entire TextField
prefixIcon	Draws one inside the TextField to the left
suffixIcon	Same as prefixIcon but to the far right

Tip   To make it a password box (Figure 4-5), set obscureText property to true. As the user types, each character appears for a second and is replaced by a dot.

```
return TextField(
  obscureText: true,
  decoration: InputDecoration(
    labelText: 'Password',
  ),
);
```

Figure 4-5. *A password box with obscureText*

Want a special soft keyboard? No problem. Just use the keyboardType property. Results are shown in Figures 4-6 through 4-9.

```
return TextField(
  keyboardType: TextInputType.number,
);
```

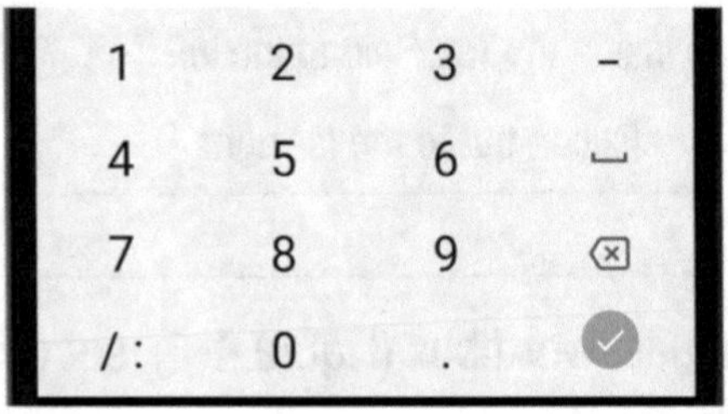

Figure 4-6. *TextInputType.datetime*

Figure 4-7. *TextInputType.email. Note the @ sign*

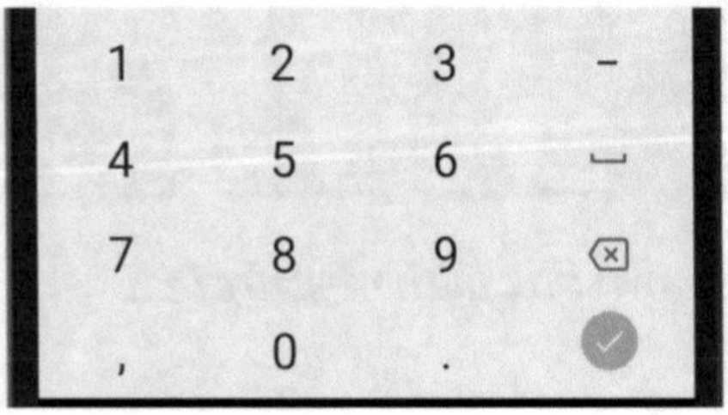

Figure 4-8. *TextInputType.number*

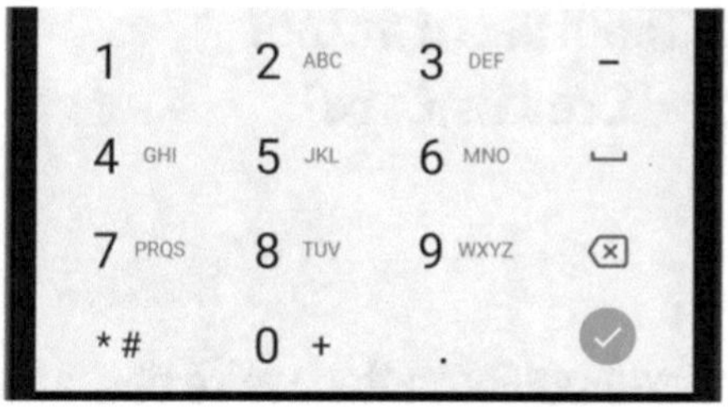

Figure 4-9. *TextInputType.phone*

Tip   If you want to limit the type of text that is allowed to be entered, you can do so with the TextInput's inputFormatters property. It's actually an array so you can combine one or more of ...

- BlacklistingTextInputFormatter – Forbids certain characters from being entered. They just don't appear when the user types.

- WhitelistingTextInputFormatter – Allows only these characters to be entered. Anything outside this list doesn't appear.

- LengthLimitingTextInputFormatter – Can't type more than X characters.

Those first two will allow you to use regular expressions to specify patterns that you want (white list) or don't want (black list). Here's an example:

```
return TextField(
  inputFormatters: [
    WhitelistingTextInputFormatter(RegExp('[0-9 -]')),
    LengthLimitingTextInputFormatter(16)
  ],
```

```
  decoration: InputDecoration(
    labelText: 'Credit Card',
  ),
);
```

In the WhitelistingTextInputFormatter, we're only allowing numbers 0–9, a space, or a dash. Then the LengthLimitingTextInputFormatter is keeping to a max of 16 characters.

Checkboxes

Flutter checkboxes (Figure 4-10) have a boolean value property and an onChanged method which fires after every change. Like all of the other input widgets, the onChanged method receives the value that the user set. Therefore, in the case of Checkboxes, that value is a bool.

```
Checkbox(
  value: true,
  onChanged: (bool val) => print(val)),
```

Figure 4-10. *A Flutter Checkbox widget*

Tip   A Flutter Switch (Figure 4-11) serves the same purpose as a Checkbox – it is on or off. So the Switch widget has the same options and works in the same way. It just looks different.

Figure 4-11. *A Flutter Switch widget*

Radio buttons

Of course the magic in a radio button is that if you select one, the others in the same group are deselected. So obviously we need to group them somehow. In Flutter, Radio widgets are grouped when you set the groupValue property to the same local variable. This variable holds the value of the <u>one</u> Radio that is currently turned on.

Each Radio also has its own value property, the value associated with <u>that</u> particular widget whether it is selected or not. In the onChanged method, you'll set the groupValue variable to the radio's value:

```
SearchType _searchType;
//Other code goes here
Radio<SearchType>(
    groupValue: _searchType,
    value: SearchType.anywhere,
    onChanged: (SearchType val) => _searchType = val),
const Text('Search anywhere'),
Radio<SearchType>(
    groupValue: _searchType,
    value: SearchType.text,
    onChanged: (SearchType val) => _searchType = val),
const Text('Search page text'),
Radio<SearchType>(
    groupValue: _searchType,
    value: SearchType.title,
    onChanged: (SearchType val) => _searchType = val),
const Text('Search page title'),
```

This simplified code would create something like Figure 4-12.

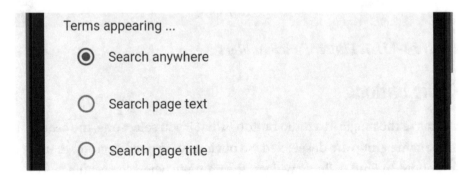

Figure 4-12. *Flutter Radio widgets*

Sliders

A slider is a handy affordance when you want your user to pick a numeric value between an upper and lower limit (Figure 4-13).

Figure 4-13. *A slider with the value of 25*

To get one in Flutter, you'll use the Slider widget which requires an onChanged event and a value property, a double. It also has a min which defaults to 0.0 and a max which defaults to 1.0. A range of zero to one is rarely useful, so you'll usually change that. It also has a label property which is an indicator telling the user what value they're choosing.

```
Slider(
  label: _value.toString(),
  min: 0, max: 100,
  divisions: 100,
  value: _value,
  onChanged: (double val) => _value = val,
),
```

Dropdowns

Dropdowns are great for picking one of a small number of things, like in an enumeration. Let's say we have an enum like this:

```
enum SearchType { web, image, news, shopping }
```

Where obviously we're defining a "SearchType" as either "web," "image," "news," or "shopping." If we wanted our user to choose from one of those, we might present them with a DropdownButton widget that might look like Figure 4-14 to start with.

Figure 4-14. *DropdownButton with nothing chosen*

Then, when they tap the dropdown, it looks like Figure 4-15.

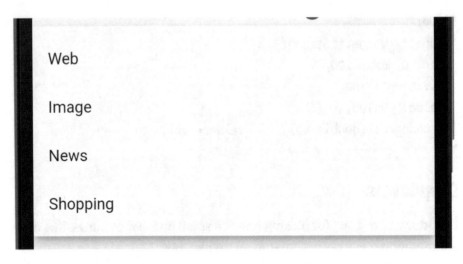

Figure 4-15. DropdownButton expanded to show the choices

And when they tap one of the options, it is chosen (Figure 4-16).

Figure 4-16. DropdownButton with an option selected

To create that DropdownButton, our Flutter code might look like this:

```
SearchType _searchType = SearchType.web;
//Other code goes here
DropdownButton<SearchType>(
  value: _searchType,
  items: const <DropdownMenuItem<SearchType>>[
    DropdownMenuItem<SearchType>(
      child:Text('Web'),
      value: SearchType.web,
    ),
```

```
    DropdownMenuItem<SearchType>(
      child:Text('Image'),
      value: SearchType.image,
    ),
    DropdownMenuItem<SearchType>(
      child:Text('News'),
      value: SearchType.news,
    ),
    DropdownMenuItem<SearchType>(
      child:Text('Shopping'),
      value: SearchType.shopping,
      ),
  ],
  onChanged: (SearchType val) => _searchType = val,
),
```

Putting the form widgets together

It's cool that we have all of these different types of fields that look good and work great. But you will often want them to be grouped together so that they can be somewhat controlled as a group. You'll do this with a Form widget.

Form widget

As with HTML, you can live just fine without a Form widget. It is a convenience widget with no visual component. That is to say you never actually see it rendered on the device. Its only purpose is to wrap all of its inputs, thereby grouping them – and their data – into a unit. It does so using a *key*. Remember that we introduced keys in the last chapter and told you that except in a few situations, keys can be ignored. This is one place where keys are needed. If you decide to use a Form, you need a GlobalKey of type FormState:

```
GlobalKey<FormState> _key = GlobalKey<FormState>();
```

You'll set that key as a property to your form:

```
@override
Widget build(BuildContext context) {
  return Form(
    key: _key,
    autovalidate: true,
    child: // All the form fields will go here
  );
}
```

At first glance, the Form doesn't seem to change anything. But a closer look reveals that we now have access to

- autovalidate: a bool. True means run validations as soon as any field changes. False means you'll run it manually. (We'll talk about validations in a few pages.)

- The key itself which we called _key in the preceding example.

That _key has a *currentState* property which in turn has these methods:

1. save()– Saves all fields inside the form by calling each's onSaved

2. validate()– Runs each field's validator function

3. reset()– Resets each field inside the form back to its initialValue

Armed with all this, you can guess how the Form groups the fields nested inside of it. When you call one of these three methods on FormState, it iterates the inner fields and calls that method on each. One call at the Form level fires them all.

But hang on a second! If _key.currentState.save() is calling a field's onSaved(), we need to provide an onSaved method. Same with validate() calling the validator. But the TextField, Dropdown, Radio, Checkbox, and Slider widgets themselves don't have those methods. What do we do now? We wrap each field in a FormField widget which **does** have those methods. (And the rabbit hole gets deeper.)

FormField widget

This widget's entire purpose in life is to provide save, reset, and validator event handlers to an inner widget. The FormField widget can wrap any widget using a builder property:

```
FormField<String>(
  builder: (FormFieldState<String> state) {
    return TextField(); // Any field widget like DropDownButton,
                        // Radio, Checkbox, or Slider.
  },
  onSaved: (String initialValue) {
    // Push values to a repository or something here.
  },
  validator: (String val) {
    // Put validation logic here (further explained below).
  },
),
```

So we first wrap a FormField widget around each input widget, and we do so in a method called *builder*. Then we can add the onSaved and validator methods.

Tip   Treat a TextField differently. Instead of wrapping it, replace it with a TextFormField widget if you use it inside a Form. This new widget is easy to confuse with a TextField but it is different. Basically ...

TextFormField = TextField + FormField

The Flutter team knew that we'd routinely need a TextField widget in combination with a FormField widget so they created the TextFormField widget which has all of the properties of a TextField but adds an onSaved, validator, and reset:

```
TextFormField(
  onSaved: (String val) {
    print('Search Term TextField: form saved $val');
  },
  validator: (String val) {
    // Put your validation logic here
  },
),
```

Now isn't that nicer? Finally we catch a break in making things easier. Checkboxes don't have this feature. Nor do Radios nor Dropdowns. None except TextFields.

Best practice: Text inputs without a Form should always be a TextField. Text inputs inside a Form should always be a TextFormField.

onSaved

Please remember that your Form has a key which has a currentState which has a save() method. Got all that? No? Not super clear? Let's try it this way; on a "Save" button press, you will write your code to call ...

```
_key.currentState.save();
```

... and it in turn invokes the onSaved method for each FormField that has one.

validator

Similarly, you probably guessed that you can call ...

```
_key.currentState.validate();
```

... and Flutter will call each FormField's validator method. But there's more! If you set the Form's autovalidate property to true, Flutter will validate immediately as the user makes changes.

Each validator function will receive a value – the value to be validated – and return a string. You'll write it to return null if the input value is valid and an actual string if it is invalid. That returned string is the error message Flutter will show your user.

Validate while typing

Remember that the way to perform instant validation is to set Form. autovalidate to true and write a validator for your TextFormField:

```
return Form(
 autovalidate: true,
 child: Container(
  TextFormField(
    validator: (String val) {
```

```
    // Let's say that an empty value is invalid.
    if (val.isEmpty)
      return 'We need something to search for';
    return null;
    },
  ),
  ),
);
```

Obviously it makes no sense to validate a DropdownButton, Radio, Checkbox, Switch, or Slider while typing because you don't type into them. But less obviously, it does not work with a TextField inside of a FormField. It only works with a TextFormField. Strange, right?

Tip   Again, best practice is to use a TextFormField. But if you insist on using a TextField inside a FormField, you can brute force set errorText like this:

```
FormField<String>(
  builder: (FormFieldState<String> state) {
    return TextField(
      controller: _emailController,
      decoration: InputDecoration(
        // This says if the value looks like an email
        set errorText
        // to null. If not, display an error message.
        errorText:
          RegExp(r'^[a-zA-Z0-9.]+@[a-zA-Z0-9]+\.
          [a-zA-Z]+')
          .hasMatch(_emailController.text)
          ? null
```

```
      : "That's not an email address",
   ),
  );
 },
),
```

Validate only after submit attempt

There are times when you don't want your code to validate until the user has finished entering data. You should first set autovalidate to false. Then call validate() in the button's pressed event:

```
RaisedButton(
 child: const Text('Submit'),
 onPressed: () {
  // If every field passes validation, run their save methods.
  if (_key.currentState.validate()) {
   _key.currentState.save();
   print('Successfully saved the state.')
  }
 },
)
```

One big Form example

I know, I know. This is pretty complex stuff. It might help to see these things in context – how they all fit together. Below you'll find a fully commented example ... a **big** example. But as big as it is, it was originally much larger. Please look at our online source code repository for the full example. Hopefully they will help your understanding of how Form fields relate.

Let's say that we wanted to create a scene for the user to submit a Google-like web search. We'll give them a TextFormField for the search String, a DropdownButton with the type of search, a checkbox to enable/disable safeSearch, and a button to submit:

```
enum SearchType { web, image, news, shopping }

// This is a stateful widget. Don't worry about how it or
// the setState() calls work until
// Chapter 9. For now, just focus on the Form itself.
class ProperForm extends StatefulWidget {
 @override
 _ProperFormState createState() => _ProperFormState();
}

class _ProperFormState extends State<ProperForm> {
 // A Map (aka. hash) to hold the data from the Form.
 final Map<String, dynamic> _searchForm = <String, dynamic>{
  'searchTerm': ",
  'searchType': SearchType.web,
  'safeSearchOn': true,
 };

 // The Flutter key to point to the Form
 final GlobalKey<FormState> _key = GlobalKey();

 @override
 Widget build(BuildContext context) {
  return Form(
   key: _key,
   // Make autovalidate true to validate on every keystroke. In
   // this case we only want to validate on submit.
   //autovalidate: true,
   child: Container(
```

```
child: ListView(
 children: <Widget>[
  TextFormField(
   initialValue: _searchForm['searchTerm'],
   decoration: InputDecoration(
    labelText: 'Search terms',
   ),
   // On every keystroke, you can do something.
   onChanged: (String val) {
    setState(() => _searchForm['searchTerm'] = val);
   },
   // When the user submits, you could do something
   // for this field
   onSaved: (String val) { },
   //Called when we "validate()". The val is the String
   // in the text box.
   //Note that it returns a String; null if validation passes
   // and an error message if it fails for some reason.
   validator: (String val) {
    if (val.isEmpty) {
     return 'We need something to search for';
    }
    return null;
   },
  ),

  FormField<SearchType>(
   builder: (FormFieldState<SearchType> state) {
    return DropdownButton<SearchType>(
     value: _searchForm['searchType'],
     items: const <DropdownMenuItem<SearchType>>[
      DropdownMenuItem<SearchType>(
```

```
        child: Text('Web'),
        value: SearchType.web,
      ),
      DropdownMenuItem<SearchType>(
        child: Text('Image'),
        value: SearchType.image,
      ),
      DropdownMenuItem<SearchType>(
        child: Text('News'),
        value: SearchType.news,
      ),
      DropdownMenuItem<SearchType>(
        child: Text('Shopping'),
        value: SearchType.shopping,
      ),
    ],
    onChanged: (SearchType val) {
      setState(() => _searchForm['searchType'] = val);
    },
  );
},
onSaved: (SearchType initialValue) {},
),
// Wrapping the Checkbox in a FormField so we can have an
// onSaved and a validator
FormField<bool>(
  //initialValue: false, // Ignored for Checkboxes
  builder: (FormFieldState<bool> state) {
    return Row(
      children: <Widget>[
        Checkbox(
```

```
    value: _searchForm['safeSearchOn'],
    // Every time it changes, you can do something.
    onChanged: (bool val) {
      setState(() => _searchForm['safeSearchOn'] = val);
    },
    ),
    const Text('Safesearch on'),
    ],
  );
},
// When the user saves, this is run
onSaved: (bool initialValue) {},
// No need for validation because it is a checkbox. But
// if you wanted it, put a validator function here.
),

// This is the 'Submit' button
RaisedButton(
  child: const Text('Submit'),
  onPressed: () {
    // If every field passes validation, let them through.
    // Remember, this calls the validator on all fields in
    // the form.
    if (_key.currentState.validate()) {
      // Similarly this calls onSaved() for all fields
      _key.currentState.save();
      // You'd save the data to a database or whatever here
      print('Successfully saved the state.');
    }
  },
)
],
```

```
        ),
        ),
      );
    }
}
```

Conclusion

It takes a while to understand Flutter forms. Please don't be discouraged.
Look over the preceding example a couple more times and write a little
code. It begins to make sense very quickly. And while the topic of Forms
might have been a little intimidating to you, Images, Icons, and Text were
very straightforward, right?

In the next chapter, we'll start to see our app come alive because we're
going to learn about creating all the different kinds of buttons and making
them – or any widget for that matter – respond to taps and other gestures!

CHAPTER 5

Responding to Gestures

We've made great progress so far! You now know what Flutter is all about. You're well-versed in how the development and debugging process works. You know why we use widgets and are pretty darn familiar with the value widgets from the last chapter. Heck, you can even create your own stateless widgets. But we're still missing a major fundamental feature: event handling.

Let's say you have a screen where the user chooses a product and puts it in their cart. They'll have to scroll up and down through a list of products (Figure 5-1). The swipe up and down to scroll is a gesture. To choose a product, they'll tap on it. That's a gesture. Then to put it in the cart, maybe we'd have them swipe right. That's a different gesture.

© Rap Payne 2019
R. Payne, *Beginning App Development with Flutter*,
https://doi.org/10.1007/978-1-4842-5181-2_5

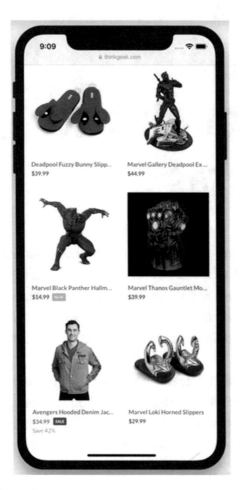

Figure 5-1. *A shopping app*

This chapter is all about handling those gestures. We'll fit gestures into two categories: gestures on built-in widgets and gestures on your custom widgets. Let's start with gesture on built-in widgets.

Meet the button family

Some gestures are super easy because they're pre-baked into certain widgets. For instance, the creators of button widgets know their sole purpose in life is to be pressed and then to do something in response to it. So all buttons come with a property called onPressed. To use it, you'll simply point it to a function to run when the user presses it:

```
Product _product;
// More code here
Widget foo() {
  return IconButton(
    icon: Icon(Icons.delete),
    onPressed: removeProduct  // The callback must return void
  );
}
// More code here
void removeProduct() {
  // Do something to remove the _product
}
```

Figure 5-2 shows the output.

Figure 5-2. *An IconButton*

You could think of a Button as the base class for all of the other buttons. It isn't really, but it wouldn't hurt for you to think of all of the others as a Button with some specialties. For instance, these are all widgets that are specialized types of buttons (Figure 5-3).

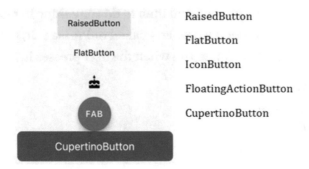

RaisedButton

FlatButton

IconButton

FloatingActionButton

CupertinoButton

Figure 5-3. *The button family*

RaisedButton

This one is simply a Button but appears like it's floating above the page. It has an elevation property to increase the simulated altitude above the page (Figure 5-4):

```
RaisedButton(
  child: Text(text: "Go"),
  onPressed: () => print("You swiped the raised button");
  elevation: 5.0
)
```

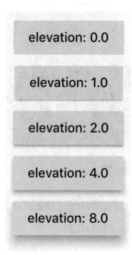

Figure 5-4. *Elevations*

FlatButton and IconButton

These are kind of the anti-RaisedButton. They just appear completely flat. They are subtle, having simple text or an icon that don't scream to be pressed, like an UNDO button or BACK button.

FloatingActionButton

This is that button you often see in the lower right of the screen. It is usually round and is an unmistakable hint to the user on how to progress to the next step in the workflow (Figure 5-5).

Figure 5-5. *Floating action button*

In Flutter, FABs are one of the three main parts of a scaffold. You'll usually see it included sort of like this:

```
Widget build(BuildContext context) {
  return Scaffold(
    appBar: AppBar(title: Text(_title)),
    body: OtherWidgetsHere(),
    floatingActionButton: FloatingActionButton(
      child: Icon(Icons.check),
      onPressed: () => {},
    ),
  );
}
```

CupertinoButton

An iOS-style button. Looks great on iPhones, but it is kind of strange to have an iOS feel on an Android device. If you use it, you must remember to add this to the top of your dart file:

```
import 'package:flutter/cupertino.dart';
```

Dismissible

Buttons are all created for one purpose: to respond to a tap. Similarly, a Dismissible is created for one purpose: to respond to a swipe. To use it, you'll usually build a list of widgets and will wrap each one with a Dismissible. When you do, each widget in the list can then respond to the swipe gesture:

```
Dismissible(
  // Give it a blue background if swiped right and
  // a red background if swiped left
  background: Container(color: Colors.blue),
  secondaryBackground: Container(color: Colors.red),
  onDismissed: (direction) {
    print("You swiped $direction");
  },
  child: SomeWidget(),
);
```

Note that as the name suggests, this is used to dismiss a widget, removing it from the view as you "swipe it away." But what if I want to swipe it but not dismiss it? This calls for a custom gesture.

Custom gestures for your custom widgets

Why does the dismissible understand the swipe gesture? Why do the buttons understand the onPressed gesture? Because the developers wrote them in. Your custom widgets will need to have gestures programmed as well. But since you're the one writing them, you get to create your own gestures. And you can create gestures that are way more interesting than a simple press. You can have your widget respond to swipes, long presses, double-presses, and pinch-to-zoom.

Tap	aka press. Includes double-tapping (tap-tap)
LongPress	Pressing on the screen for a longer time – like a second or two
Scale	aka pinching or unpinching, when you separate your fingers
Drag	aka swiping

Note: There's also a Pan, which is similar enough to a Drag that we're omitting for simplicity.

Responding to custom gestures will require these steps:

1. Decide on your gestures and behaviors.

2. Create your custom widget as normal.

3. Add a GestureDetector widget.

4. Associate your gesture with its behavior.

Step 1: Decide on your gestures and behaviors

This step is simple. Your UX expert might have already done it by the time you get ahold of the design. You simply list out the gestures you want to respond to and what they should do when that gesture is detected.

We'll work through an example. Say our user sees a list of people and has to choose the ones they like and the ones they don't. Let's have the user swipe right on each thing they like and swipe left on the ones they don't. And let's say that occasionally the user will want to add a new person between two others. We'll have them separate the two people with their fingers – kind of like making room between them for the new item. And lastly maybe we'll have the user long press to delete the person.

Gesture	Action
Swipe right	Add them to the *nice* list
Swipe left	Add them to the naughty list
Pinch (actually reverse-pinch)	Insert a new person
Long press	Delete that person

Step 2: Create your custom widget

Write the Dart code like we've learned in our past chapters. Here's a list of people:

```
class ManagePeople extends StatelessWidget {
    List<Map> fetchPeople() {
      return [
        {"first":"Jim", "last":"Halpert"},
        {"first":"Kelly", "last":"Kapoor"},
        {"first":"Creed", "last":"Bratton"},
        {"first":"Dwight", "last":"Schrute"},
        {"first":"Andy", "last":"Bernard"},
        {"first":"Pam", "last":"Beasley"},
        {"first":"Jim", "last":"Halpert"},
        {"first":"Robert", "last":"California"},
        {"first":"David", "last":"Wallace"},
        {"first":"Ryan", "last":"Howard"},
      ];
    }
```

```
@override
Widget build(BuildContext context) {
  var _peopleObjects = fetchPeople();
  return ListView(
    children: _peopleObjects.map((person) =>
      Person(person:person)).toList(),
  );
}
}
```

Step 3: Add a GestureDetector widget

The GestureDetector widget is different from most UX widgets – you can't
see it. You either wrap a GestureDetector around some widget or nest it
in the child property; it's flexible. Either way, it detects and handles the
gestures for that other widget. Since you can't see it, it's not bloated with
any properties other than child or methods other than build, just what
you'd expect. The events are where the action is!

```
return ListView(
  children: _peopleObjects
    .map((person) =>
      GestureDetector(child: Person(person: person))
    ).toList(),
);
```

Step 4: Associate your gesture with its behavior

Last step, for each event that you designed in step 1, assign a method. Now GestureDetector supports tons of events[1] so they get really confusing. We've boiled them down to the most useful ones here.

Gesture	Event(s) to use
Tap (press)	onTap
Double-tap	onDoubleTap
Long press	onLongPress
Side-to-side swipe	onHorizontalDragUpdate, Start, End
Up-and-down swipe	onVerticalDragUpdate, Start, End
Diagonal swipe	onPanUpdate, Start, End
Pinch	onScaleUpdate, Start, End

Example 1: Reacting to a long press

A long press (Figure 5-6) will ignore simple taps but will fire when the user presses for an extended time – like a second or two. Let's say our UX people decided that a long press will signal that our user wants to delete a user.

---

[1]In addition to the events we've listed, many of these gestures have advanced events for *Start, *End, *Cancel, *Up, and/or a *Down. These are a lot to take in but can be useful, so go here to read up on all of them: http://bit.ly/ FlutterGestures

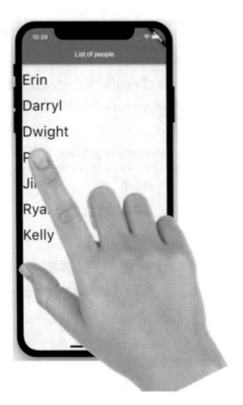

Figure 5-6. *A long press*

To make this happen, we'll add the onLongPress event handler:

```
GestureDetector(
  child: Person(person: person),
  onLongPress: () {
    _people.remove(person);
    print("Deleted ${person['first']}");
  },
);
```

Example 2: Pinching to add a new item

Let's say our UX expert suggested that users would want to add items to the list and specify where in the list they want it inserted. To communicate that, they will open the list by unpinching two items (Figure 5-7).

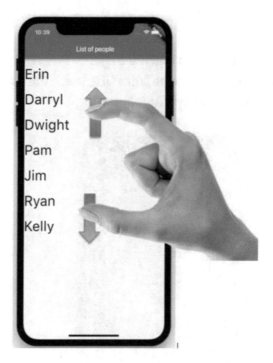

Figure 5-7. *Pinching*

We want to detect if the user was pinching in or pinching out. A normal pinch in should be ignored. But a pinch out – where they spread their fingers out – means we're adding a new person. Note that some event handlers receive in an event object. This object holds information about that particular event. In the case of a scale/pinch, it holds a property called scale. If scale is greater than 1.0, this is a pinch out. Let's say that if the user pinches out twice the normal scale, we'll assume they're wanting to add a new person to the list:

```
onScaleUpdate: (e) {
  if (e.scale > 2.0)
    addPerson(context);
},
```

Example 3: Swiping left or right

Now our UX team has decided that if the user swipes right on a person in our list, we should add them to the "nice" list, and if the user swipes left, we'll add them to the "naughty" list (Figure 5-8).

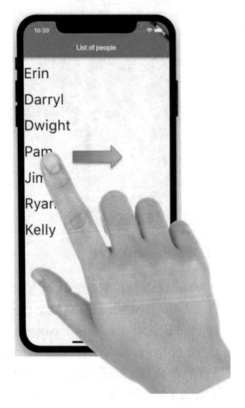

Figure 5-8. *Swiping*

To detect a swipe, we'd look for a drag or a pan. A pan is called for when we expect the user to be able to swipe <u>diagonally</u>. HorizontalDrags are only for left and right; it ignores Y-direction. VerticalDrags are only for up and down; it ignores any change in the X-direction. Since we only really care about left swipe or right swipe, we'll zero in on a HorizontalDrag gesture.

Our app can respond to any old swipe by using the onHorizontalDragEnd event. In this case we also care about the direction of the swipe; was it left to right or right to left? So we have to look at the event object in each case. At the drag start, we save the X-position of where the user's finger was. Then with every pixel move, the drag update event captures the current X-location. Finally, on drag end, we do a simple calculation; if the end X-position is greater, we know it was a swipe right. Otherwise, it was a swipe left:

```
double _swipeStartX;
String _swipeDirection;
return GestureDetector(
  child: Person(person: person),
  onHorizontalDragStart: (e) {
    _swipeStartX = e.globalPosition.dx;
  },
  onHorizontalDragUpdate: (e) {
    _swipeDirection =
        (e.globalPosition.dx > _swipeStartX) ? "Right" : "Left";
  },
  onHorizontalDragEnd: (e) {
    if (_swipeDirection == "Right")
      updatePerson(person, status: "nice");
    else
      updatePerson(person, status: "naughty");
  },
);
```

What if there are two or more gestures happening at the same time?

Let's take an example. Our user is pinching-to-zoom. The user is touching the screen, so it's a Tap. But they're also touching for a long time, so it's a LongPress. But each touch is moving, so it's a Pan. But there are two of them, so it's a Scale. What do we respond to?

The GestureDetector puts all of these in a GestureArena. (I'm not making this up!) The last gesture standing in the arena wins. If there are no listeners for a gesture, it is ejected from the arena. At any time, a gesture can quit. So in the pinch-to-zoom case, since there are two contacts and they're moving, each other gesture quits and exits the arena. The last one standing is the Scale gesture. So it's a scale.

Another example: Let's say you have onVerticalDragEnd and onHorizontalDragEnd handlers defined. When the user is finished swiping in any direction, the number of pixels is counted, and if they've moved more pixels horizontally than vertically, the onVerticalDragEnd exits the GestureArena and the onHorizontalDragEnd handler runs.

Conclusion

The bottom line is that Flutter gestures are intuitive. They work like the average developer would expect them to, making it easy for us to code and easy for our users to use. When triggered, all events will run on a separate thread so it is totally okay to have them return an Async<> object. Therefore, feel free to mark your event handling functions as async and fill them full of awaits[2].

---

[2]For more information on Futures, async, and await, take a look at Chapter 10: Your Flutter app can work with files.

CHAPTER 6

Laying Out Your Widgets

Now that we're familiar with some widgets that hold a value and how to make them respond to gestures, we are ready to make them lay out properly. In this chapter, we're going to deal with the major techniques of getting your widgets to appear on the screen in various relations to one another and to manage the space between them. Notice that I said "major techniques" not "all techniques." This is because Flutter has dozens of widgets for laying things out, many of which overlap in functionality with others. This is great if you enjoy lots of choices, but the more choices you have, the more complex a subject is.[1] So to spare you the confusion, we're not going to cover 100% of the widgets or the options. Instead we're going to focus on the ones that will get the job done in the real world without overwhelming you. We suggest that you learn the techniques in this chapter to get you 90% of what you'll ever need for layouts. Then, when you run across a situation that you can't solve with these techniques, you can do some research or call for help.

---

[1]See The Paradox of Choice at https://wikipedia.org/wiki/The_Paradox_of_Choice

© Rap Payne 2019
R. Payne, *Beginning App Development with Flutter*,
https://doi.org/10.1007/978-1-4842-5181-2_6

So to get us where we need to be, we really must know how to do five things:

1. **Layout the entire screen (aka scene)**

   This is where we'll set the look and feel of the entire app and create the structure of the scene like the title, action button, and menus (Figure 6-1).

Figure 6-1. *Title and menu appear at the top along with other things like action buttons*

2. **Position widgets above and below each other or side by side**

   When designing any scene, we break it into widgets and place them on the screen. For example, the following scene (Figure 6-2) must be broken into widgets. Since it is a scrolling list of people, we might want a bunch of PersonCard widgets (Figure 6-3) on the scene each above and below another. We'd do that with a ListView.

Figure 6-2. *A ListView can place widgets above and below each other*

Figure 6-3. *We might create a PersonCard widget*

Then in turn, each PersonCard widget should have
an image side by side with text (Figure 6-4). How do
you get the text next to the image? We'll use a Row
widget. Also notice that the text is a series of data
about that person. How do you get the text above
and below? We'll use a Column widget there.

Hildegart Israel
Email: hildegart.israel@example.com
Cell: 0175-0215028

Figure 6-4. *Row widgets and Column widgets can be used to
place things*

3. **Handle extra space in the scene**

   Hey, there's extra space on the right side of each
   Person. What if we wanted that space to be on the
   left? Or what if we wanted to put some of that extra
   space on the left of the image?

4. **Handle situations when we run out of space and
   overflow the scene**

   In the scene with all of the PersonCards, we
   have more people than we have screen so we've
   overflowed it. This normally throws an error, but
   there are several ways to fix the situation. We'll look
   at the best way.

5. **Make finer adjustments in positioning**

   Our scene currently feels crowded. What can we do
   to create a little elbow room (Figure 6-5)? Let's make
   it look a little more like in the figure:

Figure 6-5. *Fine-tuned spacing*

Alright, so there's our plan for the chapter. We'll do a deep dive into each of the five steps. But before we do, let's take just a moment to see how to debug our visual layout.

Tip   Use visual debugging to see how Flutter is making its decisions for your layout. Figure 6-6 is how your screen might look normally; when you toggle debug painting, you'll see Figure 6-7.

Figure 6-6. *Without visual debugging turned on*

Figure 6-7. *With visual debugging turned on*

All visual boxes get a teal border. Padding, margin, and border are colored in blue. Alignment/positioning is made obvious with yellow arrows. The big green arrows show widgets that can scroll. Once you get accustomed to them, these visual cues will help you see how Flutter thinks so you can tune your layout.

To turn this feature on

- In VS Code open the command palette (cmd-shift-P or control-shift-P) and type in "Toggle debug painting."

- In Android Studio/IntelliJ go to View ➤ Tool Windows ➤ Flutter Inspector and hit the "Show debug paint" button in the toolbar.

Laying out the whole scene

Here's a tip for you: Apps should never surprise their users.[2] When apps do things in the way that the user expects, they think the app is friendly, simple, and easy. Users have been trained to see a status bar at the top followed by a title bar. And while other screen affordances will vary based on need, there are definite conventions. Flutter has widgets to make your layouts feel ... well ... *normal*.

MaterialApp widget

The MaterialApp widget creates the outer framework for your app. As important as it is, the user never sees the MaterialApp because no parts of it are technically visible. It wraps your entire app, giving you the opportunity to give it a title so that when your OS moves the app into the background, it'll have a name. This is also where you'll apply the default theme for your app – fonts, sizes, colors, and so forth. We'll get way more into themes in the styles chapter. Stay tuned for that. MaterialApp is also the place to specify routes, something we'll talk much more about in the routing chapter.

Note   The "Material" in MaterialApp does indeed refer to Material Design, which is kind of a Google/Android thing. But it is probably misnamed because all apps, even iOS-focused apps, will have a MaterialApp widget at its root. It does not give your app any more of an Android feel or less of an iOS feel.

---

[2]*Don't Make Me Think* by Steve Krug is a great read on common-sense usability.

```
Widget build(BuildContext context) {
  return MaterialApp(
    home: MainWidget(),
    title: "Ch 6 Layouts",
    theme: ThemeData(primarySwatch: Colors.deepPurple),
    routes: <String, WidgetBuilder>{
      '/scene1: (BuildContext ctx) => MyWidget1(),
      '/scene2: (BuildContext ctx) => MyWidget2(),
      '/scene3: (BuildContext ctx) => MyWidget3(),
    },
    debugShowCheckedModeBanner: false,
  );
}
```

Finally, MaterialApp has a home property. Remember that your project will have lots of custom widgets. You specify which one is the startup widget by setting your MaterialApp's home property. This widget will be the root of your main scene and will therefore probably begin with a Scaffold widget. "What's a Scaffold widget," you say? Glad you asked ...

The Scaffold widget

Whereas the MaterialApp widget creates the **outer invisible** framework, the Scaffold widget creates the **inner visible** framework.

Scaffold has one purpose in life: to lay out the visible structure of your app to give it the predictable and therefore usable layout that so many other apps have. It creates, among other things:

- An AppBar for the title

- A section for the body

- A navbar at the bottom or a navigation drawer to the left

- A floating action button

- A bottom sheet – a section that is usually collapsed but can be slid up to reveal context-aware information for the scene that the user is on at that moment

```
@override
Widget build(BuildContext context) {
  return Scaffold(
    appBar: MyAppBar(),
    drawer: MyNavigationDrawer(),
    body: TheRealContentOfThisPartOfTheApp(),
    floatingActionButton: FloatingActionButton(
      child: Icon(Icons.add),
      onPressed: () { /* Do things here */},
    ),
    bottomNavigationBar: MyBottomNavBar,
  );
}
```

All parts of the Scaffold are optional. That kind of makes sense because you don't always want a floatingActionButton or a drawer or a bottomNavigationBar. Our screen designs will dictate which parts we need and which we don't.

The AppBar widget

To create a header bar at the top of the screen, use an AppBar widget (Figure 6-8). This is strictly optional. But your users are totally going to expect an AppBar for almost every app that isn't a game. You'll almost always have a title. And you may want to add an Icon at the start. An Icon is the *leading* property:

```
return Scaffold(
  appBar: AppBar(
      leading: Icon(Icons.traffic),
      title: Text("My Cool App"),
  ),
  /* More stuff here. FAB, body, drawer, etc. */
);
```

Figure 6-8. *The AppBar widget with a leading icon and a title*

One problem though. If you have the leading icon and also a navigation drawer, then Flutter can't use that space to display the hamburger menu (Figure 6-9):

```
return Scaffold(
  appBar: AppBar(
      /* No leading this time. */
      title: Text("My Cool App"),
  ),
  /* More stuff here. FAB, body, drawer, etc. */
);
```

Figure 6-9. *An AppBar without a leading icon is able to display a hamburger menu icon*

If you have a navigation drawer, you're probably going to want to omit the leading icon.

SafeArea widget

Device screens are seldom neat rectangles. They have rounded corners and notches and status bars at the top. If we ignored those things, certain parts of our app would be cut off or hidden. Don't want that? You have two choices, keep a huge database of all devices with their displayable areas and have a ton of gnarly conditional renderings. Horrible! Or use the SafeArea widget which in essence does that for you.

Simply wrap the SafeArea widget around all of your body content and let it do the heavy lifting for you. Putting it inside the Scaffold but around the body is a terrific place:

```
return Scaffold(
  drawer: LayoutDrawer(),
  body: SafeArea(
    child: MyNormalBody(),
  ),
```

```
floatingActionButton: FloatingActionButton(
  child: Icon(Icons.next),
  onPressed: () {},
),
);
```

SnackBar widget

Weird name, I know. Sounds like something delicious, but this widget is really a standard way to alert your user to something. A SnackBar (Figure 6-10) will appear at the bottom of your screen, occulting whatever is already down there and will disappear after a short time. You get to decide what the SnackBar says and you can even place a button on it for the user to take action.

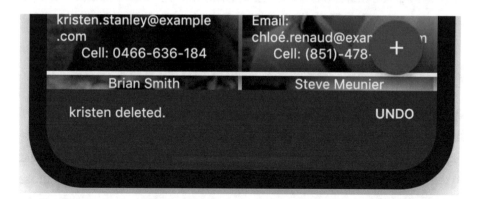

Figure 6-10. *A SnackBar shows a message and optional actions*

You can show a SnackBar in any scene you like as long as you do it in a widget that is nested inside a Scaffold:

```
GestureDetector(
  child: PersonCard(person),
  onTap: () {
    String msg = '${person['name']['first']} deleted.';
```

```
final SnackBar sb = SnackBar(
  content: Text(msg),
  duration: Duration(seconds: 5),
  action: SnackBarAction(
    textColor: Colors.white,
    label: "UNDO",
    onPressed: () {},
  ),
);
Scaffold.of(context).showSnackBar(sb);
}))
```

Note that you run the showSnackBar() method to bring the SnackBar up. You are in control of the duration that it stays up. Finally, you can add an action to the SnackBar if you want. Of course you may just want to bring up a message only with no action. It's up to you.

How Flutter decides on a widget's size

We all have constraints in life – rules and laws and boundaries we must live by. If we don't submit to those constraints, there are consequences. Flutter widgets have constraints also and they have consequences. Just like in real life, things will be easier on you if you learn the rules and how those constraints work.

In Flutter, every widget on your device's screen eventually has a height and a width which it calls the "RenderBox." Each widget also has constraints: a minHeight, a minWidth, a maxHeight, and a maxWidth which it calls the "BoxConstraints."

Note   All of these measures are in units of pixels which is obviously device-dependent. You iOS developers call them points, and Android devs call them density-independent pixels.

As long as the widget's RenderBox is completely within its BoxConstraints, life is good. In other words, its height must be between minHeight and maxHeight, and its width must be between the minWidth and maxWidth. But the moment that a widget demands to be drawn outside the constraints, bad things happen. Sometimes Flutter throws an exception, and other times it does its best and just clips the widget or shrinks it.

The dreaded "unbounded height" error

I guarantee that at some point in your career, you're going to see Flutter throw this error:

```
══╡ EXCEPTION CAUGHT BY RENDERING LIBRARY ╞═══════════
The following assertion was thrown during performLayout():
RenderFlex children have non-zero flex but incoming width
constraints are unbounded. When a row is in a parent that does
not provide a finite width constraint, for example if it is in
a horizontal scrollable, it will try to shrink-wrap its children
along the horizontal axis. Setting a flex on a child (e.g. using
Expanded) indicates that the child is to expand to fill the
remaining space in the horizontal direction. These two directives
are mutually exclusive. If a parent is to shrink-wrap its child,
the child cannot simultaneously expand to fit its parent.
```

It's not the most developer-friendly error message, is it? Most of us would have no hope of understanding the problem in our code with that error message. Similar messages may say "Vertical viewport was given unbounded height" error. Or "RenderViewport does not support returning intrinsic dimensions." None of these are very helpful. If they were being kind, they'd have said something like:

=== YOU'RE DOING IT WRONG =================================

```
The ListView you're drawing wants to be infinitely tall and it
needs a parent widget that will keep it reasonably short. Maybe
tell it to be small by wrapping it with a LimitedBox widget?
```

Now wouldn't that have been clearer? You'd understand the problem and clearly know how to fix it.

Let me help you interpret what Flutter is trying to tell us; certain widgets want to fill all of the available space that they can. In other words, they're greedy. They need a parent to constrain them. If they're inside of a parent who refuses to provide that constraint, Flutter freaks out because it can't understand what we developers are trying to do. To be blunt, this is a symptom of the developer not really understanding how Flutter handles layouts. So let me try to explain Flutter's layout algorithm in hopes of predicting and therefore avoiding snafus like the preceding example.

Note   If you don't completely understand Flutter's layout algorithm, it isn't the end of the world. You can still work with Flutter without memorizing this section. But the better understanding you have of this concept, the less frustrated you'll be when you run across layout problems in the real world. So try.

Flutter's layout algorithm

In your custom widget, you have a root widget at the top of your main method. It has branches and branches of branches and on and on. Let's call this the widget tree (Figure 6-11). Flutter has to decide how big to make each widget in the tree. It does so by asking each widget how big it would prefer to be and asking its parent if that is okay.

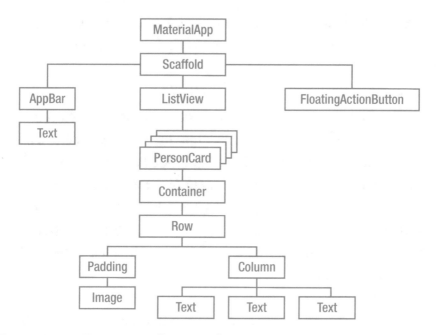

Figure 6-11. *Every scene has a widget tree*

Flutter travels down the tree starting at the root. It reads the constraint of the root widget. "What is the tallest you can be? And the widest?" It remembers them and then looks for any children. For each child, it communicates its BoxConstraints to them and then travels to the grandchildren. It keeps doing this all the way to the end of every branch. We call this the leaf level.

It then asks each leaf how big it would prefer to be. "What is your favorite height? What is your favorite width?" It allows the leaf to be drawn at its preferred size within the constraints of all of its ancestors. If the preferred size is too big, Flutter clips it at runtime – something we really try to avoid! If the preferred size is too small, Flutter pads it with extra space until it fits.

It then goes back up a level and tries to fit those branches inside their common parent which has its own constraints. And so on all the way back up to the top.

The result is that each child gets to be its favorite height and width – as long as its parent allows it. And no parent has a final size until all of its child do.

Tip   Another situation you're going to come across is when you have a widget whose RenderBox is larger than its BoxConstraints. In other words, this single widget can't fit inside its parent. The solution for that problem is occasionally a FittedBox,[3] a widget that shrinks it's child to fit. By default, you'll get a centered widget that is scaled down until it just fits both horizontally and vertically, but you have the options to align it vertically/horizontally and to stretch it or clip top/ bottom or left/right.

So you can see how we'd get the "unbounded height" error. If we had a child who tries to be as large as it can and it doesn't have a parent to tell it to stop, Flutter panics because it is now infinitely tall. To solve the problem, that child simply needs a parent to tell it to stop growing. A LimiteBox() widget's main characteristic is to do exactly that; it tells a child just how big it is allowed to get if the parent refuses to. And Flutter has a ton of widgets to control size and position. For the rest of this chapter, we're going to study the most critical of those layout widgets – the ones you absolutely must know. We'll start with Row and Colum.

Putting widgets next to or below others

Row and Column, as the names suggest, are made for laying out widgets side by side (Row, Figure 6-12) or above and below (Column, Figure 6-13). Other than how they lay out their children, they're nearly identical.

---

[3]For more details, see http://bit.ly/flutterFittedBox

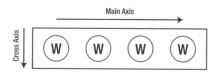

Figure 6-12. *A Row widget lays out side by side*

```
Row(
  children: <Widget>[
    Widget(),
    Widget(),
    Widget(),
    Widget(),
  ],
),
```

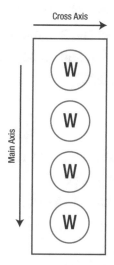

Figure 6-13. *A Column widget lays out above and below*

```
Column(
  children: <Widget>[
    Widget(),
    Widget(),
```

```
    Widget(),
    Widget(),
  ],
),
```

Notice that they both have a children property which is an array of Widgets. All widgets in the children array will be displayed in the order you add them. You can even have rows inside columns and vice versa as many levels deep as you like. In this way you can create nearly any layout imaginable in any app.

Rows and columns will be your go-to layout widgets. Yes, there are others, but these two are your first calls.

Note   Occasionally you'll want two things above and below when the device is in landscape and side by side when in portrait. So you want them in a row at times and a column at others. This is when you'll use a Flex widget which can do both. It has an orientation property that will be conditional:

```
Flex(
  direction:
    MediaQuery.of(context).orientation ==
    Orientation.landscape ?
      Axis.horizontal : Axis.vertical,
  children: <Widget>[
    SomeWidget(),
    SomeWidget(),
    SomeWidget(),
  ],
),
```

This doesn't happen as often as you might think. Use it sparingly.

Your widgets will never fit!

It would be an overwhelming coincidence if the elements fit perfectly in a scene. And if they ever fit perfectly, as soon as the app is run on a different screen size or rotated from portrait to landscape, that will change. So we need to handle two situations:

1. What if there's extra space left over? (more screen than pixels taken up by the widgets)

2. What if there's not enough space? (too many widgets in a given space)

These are both likely to happen *simultaneously* on different parts of your scene. Let's tackle leftover space first.

What if there's extra space left over?

This is an easy problem to solve. The only question you really need to answer is how to distribute the extra room. How much space do you want to allocate around each of the other widgets? You have several options. The easiest and quickest is to use mainAxisAlignment and crossAxisAlignment.

mainAxisAlignment

MainAxisAlignment is a property of the Row or Column (Figure 6-14). With it you control how the extra space is allocated with respect to the widgets along the main axis – vertical for columns and horizontal for rows:

```
child: Column(
  mainAxisAlignment: MainAxisAlignment.spaceEvenly,
  children: <Widget>[
    SubWidget(),
    SubWidget(),
```

You have a few choices:

start	end	center	spaceBetween	spaceEvenly	spaceAround
No space between them. All bunched up at the start. The default.	Same but at the end.	Same but we put space before the first and after the last	All remaining space is divided between each child widget	Same but some is saved for before the first and after the last	Same but the the spaces at the ends get half as much as the spaces between

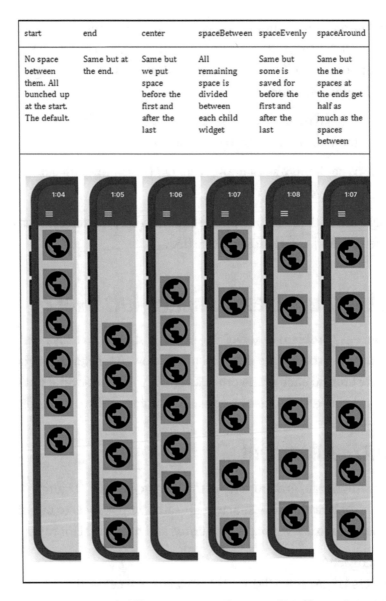

Figure 6-14. *mainAxisAlignment says how to distribute the extra space along the main axis*

crossAxisAlignment

crossAxisAlignment is also a property of the Row or Column; it decides where to put the extra space if the widgets are of different heights in a row or widths in a column (Figure 6-15). Your options are

start	end	center	stretch
Align them left in a column or top in a row	Align them right in a column or bottom in a row	Center them	Make them all the full width in a column or full height in a row

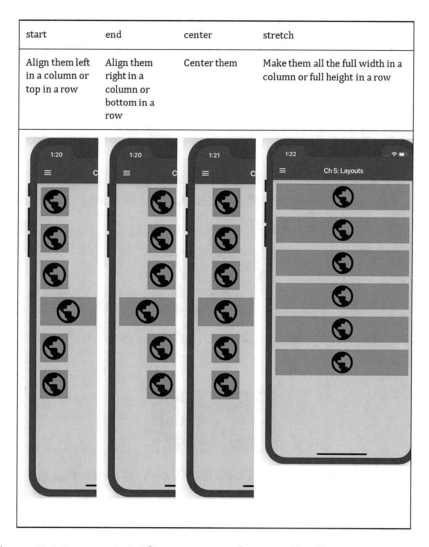

Figure 6-15. *crossAxisAlignment says how to distribute extra space along the cross axis*

There's also one more: baseline. But it only makes sense in a row, and it is much less frequently used.

Tip   If you want the children of a Column to all be the same width but not necessarily the entire width of the screen, use the IntrinsicWidth widget. With crossAxisAlignment.stretch, they all stretch to the maximum width (Figure 6-16), but wrapped in an IntrinsicWidth, they'll all be the same size as the largest widget (Figures 6-17 and 6-18).

```
child: IntrinsicWidth(
  child: Column(
    mainAxisAlignment: MainAxisAlignment.center,
    crossAxisAlignment: CrossAxisAlignment.stretch,
    children: <Widget>[ ...
```

Figure 6-16. *Without IntrinsicWidth, all members will stretch to the entire width*

Figure 6-17. *With IntrinsicWidth, they'll only be as wide as the widest member*

Figure 6-18. *With Intrinsic width and a wider member, all are made wider*

So you can see that as the width of the longest button increases, so do they all.

___

Expanded widget

mainAxisAlignment is awesome if the spacing is cut and dried – you want equal spacing somehow. But what if you don't want spacing at all? What if you want the widgets to expand to fill the remaining space? Expanded widget to the rescue (Figure 6-19).

Let's take this code for an example:

```
Row(
  mainAxisAlignment: MainAxisAlignment.spaceAround,
  children: <Widget>[
    SubWidget(),
    SubWidget(),
    SubWidget(),
    SubWidget(),
    SubWidget(),
    SubWidget(),
  ],
```

Figure 6-19. *This Row widget has lots of extra space*

117

When you wrap a Row/Column's child in an Expanded widget (Figure 6-20), it makes that child *flexible,* meaning that if there is extra space, it will stretch along the main axis to fill that space.

Here's the same thing but with an Expanded() around the second widget:

```
Row(
  mainAxisAlignment: MainAxisAlignment.spaceAround,
  children: <Widget>[
    SubWidget(),
    Expanded(child: SubWidget()),
    SubWidget(),
    SubWidget(),
    SubWidget(),
    SubWidget(),
  ],
```

Figure 6-20. *The second widget is wrapped in an Expanded*

Note that the mainAxisAlignment now makes no difference because there is no extra space. It's all eaten up by the Expanded.

What if we add another Expanded? Let's put one around the third and fourth widgets also (Figure 6-21):

```
Row(
  children: <Widget>[
    SubWidget(),
    Expanded(child: SubWidget()),
    Expanded(child: SubWidget()),
    Expanded(child: SubWidget()),
```

```
    SubWidget(),
    SubWidget(),
  ],
```

Figure 6-21. *Expandeds will divide the free space among them*

Note that the second one is now smaller because the extra space is shared with the third and fourth widgets, divided equally among them.

But wait! There's more! We can control how much space each Expanded gets. The Expanded has a property called the flex factor which is an integer. When the Row/Column is laid out, the rigid elements are sized first. Then the flexible ones are expanded according to their flex factor (Figure 6-22). In the preceding examples, the Expandeds had the default flex factor of 1 so they got an equal amount of space. But if we gave them different flex factors, they'll expand at different rates:

```
Row(
 children: <Widget>[
    SubWidget(),
    Expanded(flex: 1, child: SubWidget()),
    Expanded(flex: 3, child: SubWidget()),
    Expanded(flex: 2, child: SubWidget()),
    SubWidget(),
    SubWidget(),
  ],
```

Figure 6-22. *Expandeds have flex property to control how much extra space each gets*

Notice that the free space has still been allocated to the Expandeds but in the proportions of 1, 3, and 2 instead of evenly. So the one with a flex factor of 3 gets three times as much space as the one with a flex factor of 1.

Note   Expanded eats up all the free space. But if you want to use Expandeds but you also want there to be some space between certain children, use the Spacer or SizedBox widgets (Figure 6-23). Spacers have a flex factor that plays well with all the other flex factors along this axis. The SizedBox has height and width properties for when you want to express its size in pixels:

```
Row(
  children: <Widget>[
    SubWidget(),
    Spacer(),
    Expanded(flex: 1, child: SubWidget()),
    Spacer(flex: 2),
    Expanded(flex: 3, child: SubWidget()),
    Expanded(flex: 2, child: SubWidget()),
    SubWidget(),
    SizedBox(width: 10,),
    SubWidget(),
  ],
```

Figure 6-23. *Spacer() and SizedBox() add free space back in but put you in control as to where and how much*

What if there's not enough space?

We've tackled the situations where there is too much space and how to control where that extra space is allocated. But what if there is too *little* space? Like we are trying to squeeze too many widgets into too small a row or column? Unless you do something about it, Flutter will clip the widgets which looks terrible and worse, may hide some widgets from the user.

So what do you do? You allow scrolling!

While it is possible to scroll in both directions, it creates some serious usability issues. So we recommend that you stick to scrolling in one direction only and that it usually be vertical scrolling. The easiest way to scroll is with a ListView.

The ListView widget

ListView has actually has four different ways to use it:

1. new ListView – Normal use. It has a children property that takes a collection of static widgets.

2. ListView.builder – For dynamically creating children from a list of items.

3. ListView.separated – Like builder but also puts a widget *between* each item. Great for inserting ads in the list periodically. Read more at `http://bit.ly/flutter_listview_separated`.

4.   ListView.custom – For rolling your own advanced listviews. Read more at http://bit.ly/flutter_ listview_custom.

Let's take a look at the first two options starting with the regular ListView.

Regular ListView: When you have a few widgets to display

Generically, a ListView takes a small number of other widgets and makes it scrollable. Why a "small number"? Because this is designed to be a static list, one that you, the developer, simply types into the build() method by hand. In fact, oftentimes the way you discover you'll need a regular ListView is when your column overflows. The fix is either to remove children, resize the children, or simply change the Column to a ListView. Columns and ListViews both have a children property:

```
Widget _build(BuildContext context) {
 return ListView(
  children: <Widget>[
    FirstWidget(),
    SecondWidget(),
    ThirdWidget(),
  ],
 );
}
```

This version of ListView is great for a small number of widgets to display, but where ListView really shines is when you want to display a list of things – people, products, stores – anything you'd retrieve from a database or Ajax service. For displaying an indeterminate number of scrollable items, we'll want the ListView.builder constructor.

ListView.builder: When you're building widgets from a list of objects

ListView's alternative constructor, ListView.builder receives two parameters, an itemCount and an ItemBuilder property that is a function. This makes the ListView lazy-loaded. The itemBuilder function dynamically creates children widgets on demand. As the user scrolls close to the bottom of the list, itemBuilder creates new items to be scrolled into view. And when we scroll something far enough off the screen, it is paged out of memory and disposed of. Pretty cool.

```
Widget _build(BuildContext context) {
  return ListView.builder(
    scrollDirection: Axis.vertical,
    itemCount: _people.length,
    itemBuilder: (BuildContext context, int i) {
      return PersonCard(_peopleList[i]);
    },
  );
}
```

The itemCount property is an integer that tells us how many things we're going to draw so we usually set it to the length of the array/collection of things we're scrolling through. The itemBuilder function receives two parameters: the context and an integer which is 0 for the first item and increments each time it is run.

We've covered laying out the scene including what to do if there is extra space on the scene or there isn't enough of it. So let's cover the last of our five topics, how to fine-tune the spacing and position of widgets. We'll do this by exploring the box model.

Container widget and the box model

Flutter has borrowed heavily from other technologies including HTML and the Web which have the ideas of borders, padding, and margin. These are collectively called the box model. They're used to create pleasant-to-the-eyes spacing around and between screen elements. It's a battle-proven concept that has worked great for the Web so why not borrow it for Flutter?

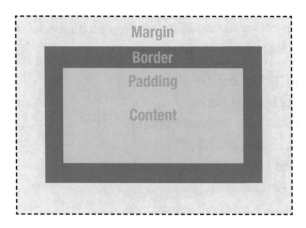

Figure 6-24. *The box model defines padding, border, and margin*

Let's say that we have a sized image that we want framed so to speak with a padding of 8, a margin of 10, and a border of 1. Flutter newcomers might try this first:

```
Image.network(
  _peopleList[i]['picture']['thumbnail'],
  padding: 8.0,
  margin: 10.0,
  border: 1.0,
),
```

This would not work since Image widgets don't have a padding, margin, or borders. But you know what does? Containers!

Web developers often apply these things by wrapping elements in a generic container called a <div> and then applying styles to create pleasant spacing for our web pages.

Flutter doesn't have a <div>, but it does have a div-like widget called a Container which ... well ... *contains* other things. In fact, its entire life purpose is to apply layout and styles to the things inside of it. An HTML <div> can hold multiple things, but a Flutter Container only holds one child. It has properties called padding, margin, and decoration. We'll leave decoration for the styles chapter, but padding and margin are awfully handy for creating nice-looking spacing:

```
Container(
  padding: EdgeInsets.all(8.0),
  margin: EdgeInsets.all(10.0),
  decoration: BoxDecoration(border: Border.all(width: 1.0)),
  child:   Image.network(thePicture),
  // Container has *lots* of other properties, many of which
  // we'll cover in the Styles chapter.
),
```

Tip   Margin and padding might have been easier to learn if they had just allowed us to list four number values representing the four sides. (They couldn't make it easy, could they?) Instead, we use a helper widget called EdgeInsets.

- EdgeInsets.all(8.0) – Same value applied to all four sides evenly.

- EdgeInsets.symmetric(horizontal: 7.0, vertical: 5.0) – Top and bottom are the same. Left and right are the same.

- EdgeInsets.only(top: 20.0, bottom: 40.0, left: 10.0, right: 30.0) – Left, top, right bottom can all be different.

- EdgeInsets.fromLTRB(10.0, 20.0, 30.0, 40.0) – Same as the preceding one but less typing.

Also note that if you want padding only – no other formatting – the Padding widget is a shorthand.

```
Container(                          Padding(
  padding: EdgeInsets.all(5),         padding: EdgeInsets.all(5),
  child: Text("foo"),                 child: Text("foo"),
),                                  ),
```

These two are equivalent.

Alignment and positioning within a Container

When you place a small child widget in a large Container, there will be more space in the Container than is needed by its child widget. That child widget will be located in the top-left corner by default. You have the option of positioning it with the *alignment* property:

```
Container(
  width: 150, height: 150,
  alignment: Alignment(1.0, -1.0),
  child:    Image.network(
    _peopleList[i]['picture']['thumbnail'],
  ),
),
```

Those alignment numbers represent the horizontal alignment (–1.0 is far left, 0.0 is center, and 1.0 is far right) and the vertical alignment (–1.0 is top, 0.0 is center, and 1.0 is bottom). See Figure 6-25.

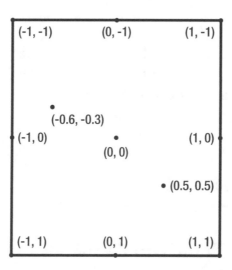

Figure 6-25. *Alignment coordinate system with 0,0 at the center*

But you will probably prefer to use English words rather than numbers when you can:

```
Container(
  width: 150, height: 150,
  alignment: Alignment.centerLeft,
  child:    Image.network(
    _peopleList[i]['picture']['thumbnail'],
  ),
),
```

Alignment can take on any of these values: topLeft, topCenter, topRight, centerLeft, center, centerRight, bottomLeft, bottomCenter, and bottomRight. Now, isn't that easier to write and easier for your fellow devs to read?

Tip   The Align widget is a shorthand for specifying the alignment and no other properties. The Center widget is merely a shorthand for centering.

```
Container(              Align(                 Center(
 alignment:             alignment:              child: Text("foo"),
  Alignment.center,      Alignment.center,      ),
 child: Text("foo"),    child: Text("foo"),
),                      ),
```

These three are equivalent.

So how do you determine the size of a Container?

You may have noticed that I tried to slip width and height by you in that last section. Yes, you can tell a Container you want it to have a particular width and height, and it will comply **when it is able**. Width and height both take a simple number that can range from zero to double.infinity. The value double.infinity **hints** to be as large as its parent will allow.

Now, I know what you're thinking. "Rap, what do you mean by 'when it is able' and 'hints'? Aren't there any hard rules? I want Container sizes to be predictable!" And I completely agree. A Container's size is tough to predict until you know its rules. So, how does it decide then?

Remember two things. First, a Container is built to *contain* a child, but having a child is optional. 99% of the time it will have a child. The other 1% of the time we use the Container to provide a background color or to create spacing for its neighbors/siblings. Second, remember that Flutter determines layout in two phases, down the render tree to determine Box Constraints and then back up to determine RenderBox (aka "size," remember?).

We go top down:

- Flutter limits max size by passing Box Constraints down into the Container from its parent.

- The Container is laid back as it tells its parent, "If my neighbors need some space, go ahead and take it. I'll be as small as you need me to."

- If height and/or width is set, it honors those up to its max size as determined by its Box Constraints. Note that it is not an error for you to list a size greater than its Box Constraints, it just won't grow any larger. This is why you can use double.infinity without error.

Tip   Setting height and width makes the Container super rigid; it locks in a size. While this is handy when you want to fine-tune your layout, the best practice is to avoid using them unless you have a darn good reason. You generally want to allow widgets to decide their own size.

Then we go bottom up:

- In the 1% of the time that it has no child, it consumes all the remaining space up to its max Box Constraint.

- But most of the time, it has a child so the layout engine looks at the child's RenderBox.

- If the child's RenderBox is bigger than my Box Constraints, it clips the child which is a big, fat problem. It's not technically an error, but it looks bad. So avoid it. When in debug mode, Flutter will draw yellow and black stripes where it has overflowed so the developer doesn't miss it.

- If the child's RenderBox is within my Box Constraints, there is leftover room so we look at the alignment property. If alignment is not set, we put it in the upper-left corner and make the container tight – it shrinks to fit the child. Leftover room is just empty. If alignment is set, it makes the container greedy. This sort of makes sense when you think about it because how will it align top/bottom/left/right if it doesn't add space by growing?

- After all this, shrink as needed to honor the margins.

Special layout widgets

Like we said at the top of the chapter, we've now covered the tools you'll need for 90% of your layout needs, but there are more. A few are worth a glance just so you know what to look for should the situation come up. These widgets are designed for very particular layout situations that, while common, aren't everyday but need specialized tools to make happen.

Stack widget

This is for when you want to layer widgets so that they overlap one another. You want to *stack* them in the Z-direction. With Stack, you'll list some number of widgets, and they'll be displayed in that order one on top of another. The last one will occult (hide) the previous one if they overlap which will occult the one before that which will overlap the one before that and so on.

I was really torn about where to cover the stack widget. On one hand, it involves laying out a screen which fits much better in this chapter. But on the other hand, Stacks excel in creating cards which is definitely a styling concept and therefore fits better in the next chapter. We decided to mention it here but really focus on it in later. So stay tuned for that.

GridView widget

Here's another thing borrowed from HTML and the Web. GridView is for
displaying a list of widgets when you want them to appear in rows and
columns but don't particularly care which rows and which columns – you
just want them to show up in a grid.

To use a GridView, you'll set its children property to the list of widgets
you want to display and it will create the grid populating across and then
wrapping to the next row, resizing its space available until it just fits. And
here's the greatest part, it automatically scrolls!

GridView has two constructors, GridView.extent() and GridView.count().

GridView.extent()

Extent refers to the maximum width of the child. GridView will only let its
kids grow to that size. If they try to get bigger, it puts another element on
that row and shrinks them all until they just fit across the entire width. Take
a look at this example:

```
Widget build(BuildContext context) {
  return GridView.extent(
    maxCrossAxisExtent: 300.0,
    children:
      people.map<Widget>((dynamic person) =>
                    PersonCard(person)).toList(),
  );
}
```

Notice in Figures 6-26 and 6-27 how the containers resize to something
less than 300. GridView decides that it can fit two across in portrait
orientation. But when rotated, those two would have resized to something
bigger than 300 so it puts three on each row.

Figure 6-26. *GridView.extent() in portrait*

Figure 6-27. *The same GridView.extent() in landscape mode*

GridView.count( )

With the count() constructor, you specify how many columns you want regardless of orientation. GridView takes care of resizing its contents to fit. In the following example, we've told GridView.count() that we want two columns regardless of the orientation and the GridView sizes its children to fit exactly two across Figures 6-28 and 6-29:

```
Widget build(BuildContext context) {
  return GridView.count(
    crossAxisCount: 2,
    children:
        people.map<Widget>((dynamic person) =>
                          PersonCard(person)).toList(),
  );
}
```

Figure 6-28. *GridView.count() in portrait orientation*

Figure 6-29. *The same GridView.count() in landscape orientation*

GridView.extent() is probably more useful because when the device is portrait, maybe you'll have two columns, but when it goes landscape, you can now fit three columns in and the contents can still fit.

The Table widget

The GridView is great when displaying widgets in rows and columns that wrap. The wrapping part means that you really don't care what children widgets end up in which row and column.

Rows and Columns are best when you <u>do</u> care in which row and column the children exist. They're rigid when you want them to be. Unfortunately, the columns can't talk to each other so they will often be misaligned (Figures 6-30 and 6-31).

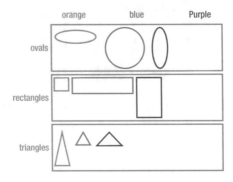

Figure 6-30. *Rows work but the columns are misaligned*

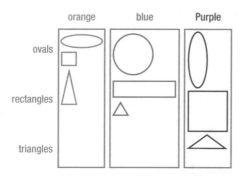

Figure 6-31. *Columns work but the rows are misaligned*

The Table widget fixes that problem. It is rigid like nested Rows and Columns, but each row and column is aware of the others and lines up nicely like GridView (Figure 6-32).

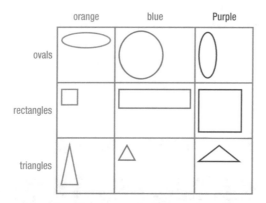

Figure 6-32. *A Table aligns the rows and columns*

Every Table widget will have children, a List of TableRow widgets. And each TableRow widget will have children, a List of widgets:

```
return Table(
  children: <TableRow>[
      TableRow(children: <Widget>[
        Text('Salesperson', style: bold,),
        Text('January', style: bold,),
```

```
        Text('February', style: bold,),
        Text('March', style: bold,),
      ]
      ),
      TableRow(children: <Widget>[
        Text('Dwight'),
        Text('3742'),
        Text('5573'),
        Text('4323'),
      ],),
      TableRow(children: <Widget>[
        Text('Phyllis'),
        Text('3823'),
        Text('4500'),
        Text('3277'),
      ],
      ),
    ],
  );
```

The preceding code would produce Figure 6-33.

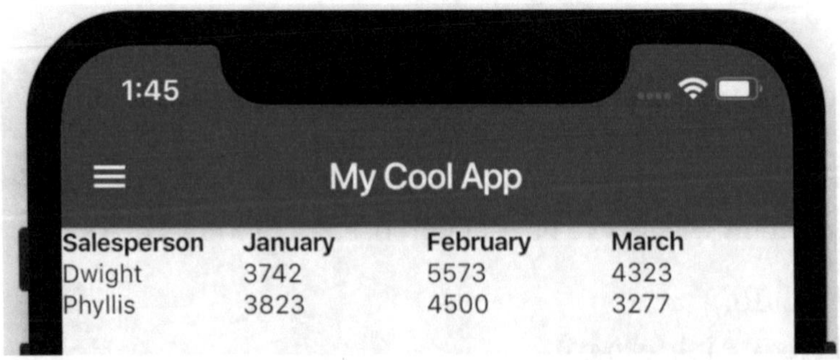

Figure 6-33. *A Table widget lines up rows and columns simultaneously*

> **Caution**   Anyone coming from an HTML background knows that you can lay out a page using HTML <table>s is possible but it is a bad idea. <table>s are for data, not for layout. Well it's the same thing in Flutter. It is possible, but generally speaking, stay away from tables for laying out a page. But if you have data, Tables are the right choice.

No matter what their contents, table columns are given equal portions of the width unless you override it with the columnWidths property. The following would give the first column 30% of the width and divide the remaining 70% evenly across the remaining columns:

```
return Table(
  columnWidths: {0: FractionColumnWidth(0.3)},
  children: <TableRow>[ ...
```

How do you span columns? Like, for a table header for example. Unfortunately, you don't with Flutter Table – yet. Stay tuned, though. There is a feature request for spanning columns.

Conclusion

I know this was a long chapter. But layouts in Flutter are not only hugely important but they're also hugely complex because of the large number of layout widgets and the way that they interact with one another. But because understanding the algorithm can save you tons of hand-wringing and head-scratching later on we thought it would be wise to cover it in depth. We hope you'll agree in the long run. After a couple more scans through this chapter and working with the widgets, we're convinced that you'll have Flutter layouts figured out.

Of course to have a complete app, you'll need to create multiple scenes and be able to navigate between them. And how do you do that? We'll cover that in the next chapter.

CHAPTER 7

Navigation and Routing

All apps have the concept of *moving* from one screen to another. The user clicks the cart button, and we go to the card screen. The user clicks "continue shopping" button, and we get to browse for more products to buy. Some app developers call it routing. Others call it navigation. Whatever you want to call it, this is one area that Flutter makes really easy because there are only four ways of navigating:

- Stacks – Each widget is full screen. The user taps a button to go through a predefined workflow. History is maintained, and they can travel back one level by hitting a back button.

- Drawers – Most of the screen shows a widget, but on the left edge, a drawer is peeking out at the user. When they press it or swipe it right, it slides out revealing a menu of choices. Pressing one changes the widget in the main part of the screen.

- Tabs – Some room is reserved for a set of tabs at the top or the bottom of the screen. When you press on a tab, we show the widget that corresponds to that tab.

© Rap Payne 2019
R. Payne, *Beginning App Development with Flutter*,
https://doi.org/10.1007/978-1-4842-5181-2_7

- Dialogs – While these aren't technically part of navigation, they are a way to see another widget, so we'll allow it. Dialogs are modal (aka pop-up windows) that stay until the user dismisses them.

Each of these methods depends on your app having a MaterialWidget as its ancestor. Let's drill into them starting with stack navigation.

Stack navigation

If you're an experienced developer, you're familiar with queues and stacks. If not, let me explain briefly. Let's say you work in a kitchen. As plates are cleaned, they're stacked, right? Each plate is put on the top of the stack. This is called *pushing* onto the stack. When it is time to serve some food, you naturally take the last plate added, the one on top of the stack. This is called *popping* off the top of the stack.

Flutter's navigation works with stacks. When you want to send the user to a new scene, you will push() a widget on the top of the stack and the user sees that widget. Each time you push(), you're making the stack of scenes taller and taller. When you are ready for them to go back to where they were before, you'll pop() the last scene off the top of the stack, and what is revealed? The previous scene.

With Flutter's stack, you'll typically predefine the scenes (aka routes) and give each a name. This must be done at the MaterialApp level like so:

```
Widget build(BuildContext context) {
  return MaterialApp(
    title: 'Shopping App',
    initialRoute: '/',
    routes: {
      '/': (BuildContext ctx) => LandingScene(),
      '/browse': (BuildContext ctx) => Browse(),
      '/product': (BuildContext ctx) => ViewProduct(),
```

```
        '/checkout: (BuildContext ctx) => Checkout(),
    },
  );
}
```

Note that with routing, we no longer use the home property. Instead, use the intialRoute property.

Tip   If your initialRoute is "/", you can omit it altogether and Flutter assumes it is "/".

Navigating forward and back

To navigate the user to a scene manually, you'll Navigator. pushNamed(context, route) and Navigator.pop(context).

To push a user to another route:

```
RaisedButton(
  child: const Text('Check out'),
  onPressed: () => Navigator.pushNamed(context, '/checkout),
),
```

Once they're finished and want to go back:

```
RaisedButton(
  child: const Text('Go back'),
  onPressed: () => Navigator.pop(context),
),
```

But wait, there's more! Notice that if you have a Scaffold, a back arrow is automatically added to the appbar (Figure 7-1). When tapped, it works to go back. And if your user is on Android, the ubiquitous Android back button works also (Figure 7-2).

Figure 7-1. *The back arrow in the appbar*

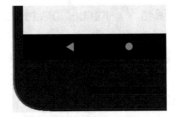

Figure 7-2. *The Android back button works with stacks*

Tip   There is another flavor of routing that doesn't use a predefined routing table in your MaterialApp. Instead, you generate the route on the fly:

```
Navigator.push<void>(context, MaterialPageRoute
<void>(builder: (BuildContext context) =>
SecondRoute());
```

As you can see, it's quite a bit more complex. But it is popular if you want custom transitions or just don't want predefined routes.

Get result after a scene is closed

With stack navigation, every pop() returns to its caller. Therefore, it is possible to return a value from each scene. This isn't extremely common, but it can be super useful when you're moving the user through a workflow. Let's say you have a section of your app that maintains a user object. The user object is defined in MyUserWidget, and we provide one button to modify the login credentials, another to modify the phone number, and yet another to modify the Twitter handle. When the user taps each button, we might push() them to a route where they change the data. If so, we'll need to return that changed data to the MyUserWidget. We'd push() a little differently having a variable receive the returned value:

```
// The 'async' is needed here because we are 'await'ing below.
onPressed:  () async {
  _user.twitterHandle =
          await Navigator.pushNamed(context, '/twitter');
},
```

Note   the *await* keyword implies that pushNamed() returns a Future. Also note that any value returned from this route will be assigned to _user.twitterHandle.

So how does this value get returned? In the pop() of course!

```
Navigator.pop<String>(context, twitterHandle);
```

Navigator.pop() is overloaded. If you add a second parameter, it will be returned to the widget that called push() in the first place. In the preceding example, twitterHandle will be returned.

Apps that are shallow work great with push() and pop(). But your app may have a deep navigation tree with lots of choices. Apps like that aren't usually best served by having umpteen buttons to push() and pop(). Instead, they should have a navigation menu. Flutter provides us with two types. Simpler apps can have tabs. More complex apps will have drawers. Let's look at drawers next.

Drawer navigation

Drawers are great when we have a lot of navigation choices – too many choices to fit in a tab. In a lot of responsive web sites, you'll see a menu across the top of the page with links to other pages on the site. Then when the site is viewed on a small device or even a narrow browser, that menu is replaced by a hamburger menu that, when clicked, will drop down a menu filled with the same choices. Basically, this is the site responding to limited screen real estate, providing menu choices that are hidden until the user asks for them.

Since most phones already have limited screen real estate, you may opt to put your menu choices in a drawer that doesn't gobble up that precious screen real estate until the user is ready to see them (Figure 7-3). When he or she is ready, they'll hit the now-familiar hamburger menu (that icon with three lines) and the choices slide out from the left (Figure 7-4). When the user chooses one, we'll Navigator.push() them to a new route.

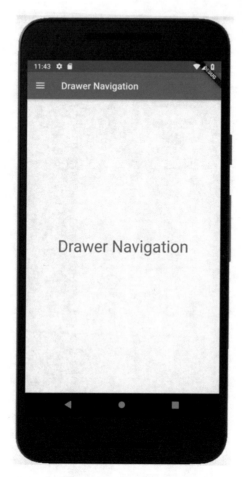

Figure 7-3. *A scene with the drawer closed*

Figure 7-4. *A scene with the drawer open*

The Drawer widget

You'll need a Drawer widget, a built-in Flutter widget that has the ability to slide out, slide in, and contain menu choices. When you use a drawer, you always include it in a Scaffold's drawer property, like this:

```
Widget build(BuildContext context) {
  return Scaffold(
    appBar: AppBar(
```

```
      title: const Text('Drawer Navigation'),
    ),
    body: const Text('DrawerNavigation'),
    drawer: Drawer(child: ListView(
      children: <Widget>[
        Text('Option 1'),
        Text('Option 2'),
        Text('Option 3'),
      ],
    ),),),
  );
}
```

Notice that when you have a drawer in your Scaffold, its hamburger icon replaces the appbar's back button. You can't see both buttons simultaneously unless you create your own buttons manually. So while drawer navigation and stack navigation *can* work together, it can be kind of awkward if you're not careful. One example of them working really well together is to have a Drawer at the topmost level, and then use stack navigation at all levels below that.

Tip   Do you want a consistent drawer to be available across your entire app? If so, we generally put a Scaffold on every scene and include the drawer in it. Therefore, it is best to put your Drawer in its own widget and include it:

```
return Scaffold(
    appBar: AppBar(
      title: const Text('Drawer Navigation'),
    ),
  body: const Text('DrawerNavigation'),
  drawer: MyDrawer(),
);
```

Filling the drawer

Adding the drawer is easy. The trick is getting entries into the drawer and then making them navigate to another widget. Note that Drawer has a *child* property that accepts a single widget. To get multiple children in your drawer, you will use a widget that supports them such as Column (doesn't scroll) or ListView (scrolls).

Whichever you choose, you'll want to put something that is tappable because to navigate, you're going to call Navigator.push() or Navigator. pushNamed() just like you did with stack navigation.

Tip   There's a cool widget called a DrawerHeader that is built to take up a large area at the top of the drawer. It is great for putting your logo or other branding information to sort of remind the user what app they are in. It is cosmetic only but it really does look cool.

```
return Drawer(
  child: ListView(
    children: <Widget>[
      DrawerHeader(
        child: Stack(
          children: <Widget>[
            Image.asset(
              'lib/assets/images/BrandLogo.jpg',
            ),
            Container(
                alignment: Alignment.bottomRight,
                child: Text(
                  'My Brand',
                  style: Theme.of(context).textTheme.display1,
                )),
```

```
          ],
        ),
      ),
      ListTile(
        leading: const Icon(Icons.looks_one),
        title: const Text('Widget 1'),
        onTap: () {
          Navigator.pushNamed(context, '/widget1');
        },
      ),
      ListTile(
        leading: const Icon(Icons.looks_two),
        title: const Text('Widget 2'),
        onTap: () {
          Navigator.pushNamed(context, '/widget2');
        },
      ),
      ListTile(
        leading: const Icon(Icons.looks_3),
        title: const Text('Widget 3'),
        onTap: () {
          Navigator.pushNamed(context, '/widget3');
        },
      ),
    ],
  ),
);
```

Drawer navigation is great and all, but UX experts have a few problems with it. They claim[1] that it drastically reduces the usability of apps, making your app less discoverable and more difficult. They say the problem is that

---

[1]http://bit.ly/HamburgerNav

the options are hidden until the user asks for them. Their objection could be resolved with an affordance that is always visible. Speaking of which ...

Tab Navigation

As you would imagine, a tab system matches N tabs with N widgets. When the user presses tab 1, they see widget 1 and so forth (Figure 7-5). The matching is done with a TabBar widget, a TabBarView widget, and a TabBarController.

Figure 7-5. *A tabbar at the top and at the bottom*

TabController

The TabController is the least obvious part. Just know that you have to have one or you get the error in Figure 7-6.

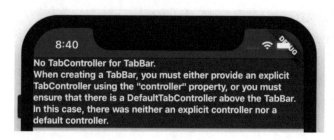

Figure 7-6. *When you forget a TabController*

The easiest way to create one is to wrap everything in a DefaultTabController() with a length property. Problem solved. This part is pretty simple – so simple you may wonder why Flutter doesn't create one implicitly for you. If you were thinking that, you wouldn't be wrong:

```
Widget build(BuildContext context) {
  return DefaultTabController(
    length: 3,
    child: Scaffold(
    ...
  );
}
```

TabBarView

Next you'll want to add a TabBarView widget. This holds the widgets that will eventually be shown when the user presses a tab, defining where they will be shown. Usually this is the entire rest of the screen, but you have the opportunity to put widgets above the TabBarView or below it or really anywhere around it:

```
child: Scaffold(
  body: TabBarView(
    children: <Widget>[
      WidgetA(),
      WidgetB(),
      WidgetC(),
    ],
  ),
```

TabBar and Tabs

Lastly we define the tabs themselves. Tabs can either hold text or an icon or both. Here's a TabBar with three tabs, each having both an icon and text:

```
child: Scaffold(
  appBar: AppBar(
    title: const Text('Tab Navigating'),
    bottom: TabBar(
      tabs: const <Widget>[
          Tab(icon: Icon(Icons.looks_one), child:Text('Show A')),
          Tab(icon: Icon(Icons.looks_two), child:Text('Show B')),
          Tab(icon: Icon(Icons.looks_3), child: Text('Show C')),
      ]),
  ...
```

Caution   There's a one-to-one correspondence between each tab and each TabBarView child; they are matched positionally. You must have the same number of tabs as you do widgets inside the TabBarView.

TabBar at the bottom

Note that previously we chose to put the TabBar in the appBar, which of course appears at the top of the screen. But sometimes your design calls for the tabs to appear at the bottom of the screen. That's easy because the Scaffold has a property called bottomNavigationBar and it is built to hold a TabBar:

```
child: Scaffold(
  ...
  bottomNavigationBar: Material(
    color: Theme.of(context).colorScheme.primary,
    child: TabBar(tabs: const <Widget>[
      Tab(icon: Icon(Icons.looks_one), child: Text('Show A')),
      Tab(icon: Icon(Icons.looks_two), child: Text('Show B')),
      Tab(icon: Icon(Icons.looks_3), child: Text('Show C')),
    ]),
  ),
),
```

> **Note**   The TabBar has the normal appearance of light text on a dark background. Thus, when you place the TabBar on top of a light background, it may be difficult to see the text (light on light). To fix this, wrap your TabBar in a Material widget with a darker background color as we did earlier.

The Dialog widget

Our last navigation category is arguably not a navigation category at all – dialogs. In one sense, you're showing another widget so ... navigation? But in another sense, you're basically showing a pop-up so ... not navigation. ¯_(ツ)_/¯

Either way, dialogs are a common thing and we should cover them. Since they don't fit well anywhere else in the book, let's pretend for the moment that they are a navigation topic. Hey, work with me here.

showDialog() and AlertDialog

showDialog() is a built-in Flutter method. You must supply a context and a builder method that returns a Widget, usually either SimpleDialog or AlertDialog. The AlertDialog has an *actions* parameter – a List of (typically) FlatButtons that let the user dismiss the dialog (Figure 7-7).

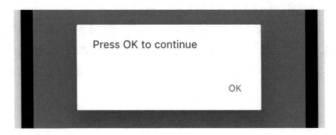

Figure 7-7. A simple AlertDialog

```
RaisedButton(
  child: const Text('I am a button. Press me'),
  onPressed: () => showDialog<void>(
    context: context,
    builder: (BuildContext context) {
      return AlertDialog(
        content: const Text('Press OK to continue'),
        actions: <Widget>[
          FlatButton(
              child: const Text('OK'),
              onPressed: () => Navigator.pop(context)),
        ],
      );
```

```
    },
  ),
),
```

This looks more complex than it needs to be. And this is the simplest form! It gets more complex if you want to give the user choices.

Responses with a Dialog

showDialog() returns a Future<T> which means that you can have it return a value to its caller. Let's pretend you want the user to respond with yes or no (Figure 7-8).

Figure 7-8. *AlertDialog that returns a value*

You might create the dialog and handle the response like this:

```
RaisedButton(
  child: const Text('Get a response'),
  onPressed: () async {
    // The builder returns the user's choice here.
    // Since it is a Future<String>, we 'await' it to
    // convert it to a String
    String response = await showDialog<String>(
```

155

```
      context: context,
      builder: (BuildContext context) {
        return AlertDialog(
          content: const Text('Are you sure?'),
          actions: <Widget>[
            FlatButton(
                child: const Text('Yes'),
                // Return "Yes" when dismissed.
                onPressed: () => Navigator.pop(context, 'Yes')),
            FlatButton(
                child: const Text('No'),
                // Return "No" when dismissed.
                onPressed: () => Navigator.pop(context, 'No')),
          ],
        );
      },
    );
    // Do things with the response that we 'await'ed above.
    print(response);
  },
),
```

Tip   As the name suggests, the SimpleDialog widget is a simpler version of the AlertDialog. It doesn't have actions and has fewer constructor parameters like titleTextStyle, contentTextStyle, and the like. Use it mainly if you don't need the user to respond to the prompt but simply to inform.

Navigation methods can be combined

While you can stack navigate to a widget with a drawer and from there to a widget with a tab, you should be careful. The methods are not incompatible, but, boy, they can get complex when mixed! For example, if you stack navigate via push() to a widget with a drawer, the back button in the appbar is no longer available. Android has a soft back button at the bottom, but iOS does not. So the user is now stuck with no way to return. Another example, a TabBarView has widgets, but these are hosted so to speak so they should have no Scaffold. If you tried to navigate to that same widget using either of the other two methods, you have no way to get back ... no drawer to show and no back button to tap. Again, the user is stuck.

We recommend sticking to just two different types and keeping the levels consistent. For example, it is pretty common to have a tabbed navigation experience for the user, and within each tab, you'll work with stack navigation. But get much more complex than that and you may get your hands full.

CHAPTER 8

Styling Your Widgets

Styling your widgets isn't entirely new to you. We've touched on some minor styling features in prior chapters, and you've seen styling techniques in our code samples. But this is the chapter where we'll take a deep dive on styling. Finally! We get to make our widgets look great in addition to merely working great.

We covered layouts in Chapter 6, "Laying Out Your Widgets," so we know how to set the location and sizes of our widgets. That's not styling. Styling is the other stuff that affects the appearance of widgets. Things like:

- Colors
- Text appearance (fonts, weights, underlines, etc.)
- Borders (thicknesses, patterns, corner radii)
- Background images
- Applying shapes to a Container

We'll discuss these along with a couple of Flutter widgets where there is considerable overlap between layout and styling: Cards and Stacks. Lastly, we'll talk about the best practice of applying default styles en masse using Themes.

But first a few words about the philosophy of styles in Flutter.

© Rap Payne 2019
R. Payne, *Beginning App Development with Flutter*,
https://doi.org/10.1007/978-1-4842-5181-2_8

Thinking in Flutter Styles

You've probably seen that Flutter has borrowed the best ideas from Android, iOS development, and web development, especially from React and the dynamicness of JavaScript. But it doesn't copy their techniques exactly. Flutter does things its own way, and it is a mistake to take the web analogies too far. It's to our benefit to grasp how Flutter is different.

First, Google has made Material Design[1] very popular in Android development and all across the Web. And while Flutter's default look conforms to Material Design, don't let anyone tell you that you're forced to use it. That's a popular but untrue misconception.

Second, Flutter's styling is not CSS. Whereas CSS has certain properties that are passed down to their children, Flutter styles are not inherited. You cannot set a font family on your custom widget for example, and have all of the Texts and TextFields and buttons beneath it suddenly begin rendering with that font. To make that kind of thing happen, it is possible to use Themes which we'll show you how to do at the end of this chapter.

Finally, Flutter, like Dart, is very verbose – it takes a lot of code to express something you'd think should be simple. And unsurprisingly, styling is no different. Just rest assured that some very smart people have written Flutter and have darn good reasons for it being as wordy as it is, safety and completeness being just two. It's a fact of life. We just want you to be aware and prepared for it.

---

[1]Material Design is a set of guidelines for the look and feel of an app. Briefly, it tries to make the UI resemble the physical world, specifically paper elements stacked on top of one another. You can read more about it at `https://material.io/`

A word about colors

Most Flutter styles are very narrowly applied; they only make sense for certain tightly defined situations. On the other hand, colors are applied nearly everywhere (Figure 8-1). Borders, text, backgrounds, icons, buttons, and shadows all have colors. And they're all specified in the same manner. For example, here's white Text in a red container with a yellow border, and all of those widgets are colored identically with the syntax "color: Colors. somethingOrOther":

```
child: Container(
  child: Text(
    'Colors!',
    style: TextStyle(color: Colors.white,),
  ),
  decoration: BoxDecoration(
      color: Colors.red,
      border: Border.all(
        color: Colors.yellow,
      )),
),
```

Figure 8-1. *Colors are everywhere in Flutter*

And you see those colored blocks in the background? Those were created like this:

```
List<Widget> _randomColors() {
  Random rnd = Random();
  return List.generate(25,
    (int i) => Container(
     color: Color.fromRGBO(
      rnd.nextInt(255), rnd.nextInt(255), rnd.nextInt(255), 1.0),
     ));
}
```

So you can create any of the 16+ million colors with Color. fromRGBO(red, green, blue, opacity) where each of the three RGB colors is a number between 0 and 255 and the opacity is 1.0 for fully opaque and 0.0 for fully transparent.

If you come from a web background, you might be more comfortable creating colors using hex numbers. This works also:

```
color: Color(0xFFFF7F00),
```

Caution   Be careful. That hex number is actually "ARGB" where the first two hexadecimal characters are the alpha channel. If you forget it, like Color(0xFFF700), you'll be painting it full transparent and you'll never see it. Just remember that if your colors don't show up, take that typical web hex number and put an "FF" in front of it.

Styling Text

There are two topics regarding the appearance of Text: TextStyle and Custom Fonts. We'll deal with these in the following page or two but stay tuned until the end of the chapter where we'll be dealing with a better way of setting those properties – Themes.

TextStyle

Text widgets have a *style* property which takes a TextStyle object (Figure 8-2).

Without TextStyle	With TextStyle

```
Widget build(BuildContext ctx){
 return Scaffold(
  body: Center(
   child: Text("Hello world "),
   ),
 );
}
```

```
Widget build(BuildContext ctx){
 return Scaffold(
  body: Center(
   child: Text(
    "Hello world" ,
    style: TextStyle(
    color: Colors.blue,
    decoration:
     TextDecoration .lineThrough,
    fontFamily: "Courier" ,
    fontSize: 34.0 ,
    fontStyle: FontStyle .italic,
    fontWeight: FontWeight .bold,
    ),
   ),
  ),
 );
}
```

Figure 8-2. *With and without style*

You'll simply set the *style* property to an instance of a TextStyle widget and set properties. TextStyle supports about 20 properties. Here are the most useful:

- color – Any of the valid 16+ million colors

- decoration – TextDecoration.underline, overline, strikethrough, none

- fontSize – A double. The number of pixels tall to make the characters. Default size 14.0 pixels

- fontStyle – FontStyle.italic or normal

- fontWeight – FontWeight.w100-w900. Or bold (which is w700) or normal (which is w400)

- fontFamily – A string

fontFamily is a bigger topic. There are some fonts that are built-in like Courier, Times New Roman, serif, and a bunch more. How many more? It depends on the type of device on which the app is running. Since we don't have control over the users' devices, the best practice is for you to stick to the default font family unless you install and use a custom font. Let's talk about how to do that.

Custom fonts

Certain designers call for custom fonts when they design scenes. It turns out with Flutter, using custom fonts is easy to implement, and they work cross-platform. It involves three steps:

1. Download the custom font files which are in ttf, woff, or woff2 format. These are customarily stored in a root-level folder called fonts, but the name is up to you (Figure 8-3).

Figure 8-3. *Fonts are usually stored in a folder called fonts*

Tip   You can find some excellent and free fonts at `http://fonts.google.com`. Search through them by type, see samples, and download them easily.

---

1. Add the font files to the pubspec.yaml file under flutter/fonts so that the compiler is notified to bundle them in the installation file.

```
flutter:
  fonts:
    - family: MrDafoe
      fonts:
        - asset: fonts/MrDafoe-Regular.ttf
    - family: NanumBrushScript
      fonts:
        - asset: fonts/NanumBrushScript-Regular.ttf
```

2. Use the case-insensitive font name in the fontFamily property of the TextStyle widget like we talked about in the previous section:

```
Text(loremIpsums[0]),   // Unstyled
Text(loremIpsums[1],    // Some, like Courier may be
                        built-in
    style: TextStyle(fontFamily: 'Courier'),),
Text(loremIpsums[2],
    style: TextStyle(fontFamily: 'NanumBrushScript'),),
Text(loremIpsums[3],
    style: TextStyle(fontFamily: 'MrDafoe'),),
```

The example above might look like Figure 8-4.

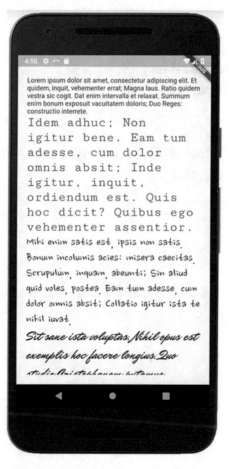

Figure 8-4. *Available fonts*

Container decorations

How do you add borders to Text? You can't. How about a background to an Icon? Nope. They don't have the capacity to have those decorations. But you know what does? A Container. When you have styling problems like these, the answer is almost always to wrap widgets in a Container and put a decoration on the Container.

Containers have a catch-all styling property called *decoration*. Here's an example of how to put a shadow on a container:

```
child: Container(
  width: 300.0,
  height: 300.0,
  decoration: BoxDecoration(
    color: Colors.purple,
    boxShadow: [
      BoxShadow(
        offset: Offset.fromDirection(0.25*pi, 10.0),
        blurRadius: 10.0,
      )
    ],
  ),
),
```

Figures 8-5 and 8-6 show boxes without and with shadows.

Figure 8-5. *Without a box shadow*

Figure 8-6. *With a box shadow*

And this is a terrific example of the wordiness with Flutter. In the Web, this would have been done in 17 characters. But in Flutter we have to remember that boxShadow is an <u>array</u> of BoxShadows, each of which has an offset which takes a direction expressed in radians, a size expressed in pixels, and the blur radius is in pixels also. Sheesh!

Blur radius may call for additional explanation. The blur radius is the distance over which the shadow dissipates. It's like putting a lampshade on a lamp. Without a shade, the light is harsh and shadows are crisp. With a lampshade, the light is softer and the shadows are also. The larger the blur radius, the softer the shadow.

Caution   You cannot specify a color directly on a Container if you're also using a BoxDecoration. But don't panic; BoxDecoration also has a color property. Just move your Container's color property into the BoxDecoration for the same effect.

There are a number of other decorations available. Let's look at the most useful ones, border, borderRadius, and BoxShape.

Border

Just like you used a BoxDecoration for shadows, you also use them to put a border on a container. Here's a red border with four different widths (Figure 8-7):

```
decoration: BoxDecoration(
  color: Colors.purple,
  border: Border(
    top: BorderSide(
      width: 10,
      color: Colors.red,
    ),
    right: BorderSide(
      width: 20,
      color: Colors.red,
    ),
    bottom: BorderSide(
      width: 30,
      color: Colors.red,
    ),
```

```
    left: BorderSide(
      width: 40,
      color: Colors.red,
    ),
  ),
),
```

Figure 8-7. *Borders with different widths*

While it's nice that Flutter allows us to have different widths and even different colored borders, how often will you use that? Usually all four sides will be uniform. So we commonly use the shorthand Border.all():

```
decoration: BoxDecoration(
  color: Colors.purple,
  border: Border.all(
    width: 10,
    color: Colors.red,
  ),
),
```

Much simpler. Yes, still verbose, but simpler.

BorderRadius

Rounded corners are a favorite look. You can make a Container rounded even if it doesn't have a border (Figure 8-8). You do this with BorderRadius:

```
decoration: BoxDecoration(
  color: Colors.purple,
  borderRadius: BorderRadius.only(
    topLeft: Radius.circular(20.0),
    topRight: Radius.circular(60.0),
  ),
),
```

Figure 8-8. *BorderRadius on two corners*

We only gave it a topLeft and a topRight radius, but there is also a bottomLeft and bottomRight property. And although we appreciate the flexibility, it is not typical to use it. We ordinarily specify all four the same (Figure 8-9):

```
decoration: BoxDecoration(
  color: Colors.purple,
  borderRadius: BorderRadius.all(
```

```
      Radius.circular(20.0),
    ),
  ),
```

Figure 8-9. *BorderRadius on all four corners*

BoxShape

Your containers don't have to always be rectangles. When you need it to be another shape, you can make it so with BoxShape or CustomPainter. BoxShape is much easier to use, but it only supports circles, as in Figure 8-10 (in addition to the default rectangle, of course):

```
Container(
  decoration: BoxDecoration(
    shape: BoxShape.circle,
    color: Colors.deepOrange,
  ),
),
```

Figure 8-10. *BoxShape.circle makes your Container round*

CustomPainter is way more complex, but it allows infinite shapes. It would be distracting to get too deep into the details of CustomPainter (Figure 8-11), but here's a quick example, a Superman shield:

```
Container(
  child: CustomPaint(
    size: Size(200, 200),
    painter: SupermanShieldPainter(),
  ),
)

class SupermanShieldPainter extends CustomPainter {
  @override
  void paint(Canvas canvas, Size size) {
    canvas.drawPath(Path()
    ..moveTo(25, 0)
    ..lineTo(125, 0)
    ..lineTo(150,25)
    ..lineTo(75, 125)
    ..lineTo(0,25)
    ..lineTo(25,0),
    Paint()
    ..style=PaintingStyle.fill
```

```
    ..color = Colors.red
  );
}
@override
bool shouldRepaint(SupermanShieldPainter oldDelegate) => false;
}
```

Figure 8-11. *Using a CustomPainter*

See? Quite a bit more involved. Note that your container is still a rectangle. It's just that the background is different. To dive deeper into CustomPainter, take a look at https://api.flutter.dev/flutter/widgets/CustomPaint-class.html.

Tip   All of these decorations are applied to the decoration property, but they also apply to a property called foregroundDecoration which, as the name suggests, is applied on a layer <u>above</u> the container. The same decorations apply there. But because they're drawn on top of the other things, you'll want to keep in mind one more modification: opacity. Colors can be made semi-transparent. The following would create a red layer on top of a container that is 50% transparent:

```
foregroundDecoration: BoxDecoration(
  color:Colors.red.withOpacity(0.5),
),
```

Stacking widgets

If you ever want two or more things to occupy the same x- and y-position on the screen, reach for the Stack widget. The stack widget enables us to lay down a widget and then put another widget in front of it and another one in front of that one and so on. Obviously the ones added later will have a higher z-index, thereby "occulting" (hiding) the one behind it. Basically it allows you to ... well ... stack the inner widgets.

Using a Stack, you can create some really cool layouts. In fact, Material Cards rely on Stacks a lot because they embrace background images with text on top of it. Maybe we want a card with a person's profile pic with their name and info superimposed on top (Figure 8-12).

Figure 8-12. *A Card with text on top of an image thanks to a Stack widget*
Image for Figures 8-12 through 8-14 courtesy Hosein Hakimi on Unsplash.com

Here's how we might accomplish that:

```
Card(
  child: Stack(
    children: <Widget>[
      Image.asset("6.jpg"),
      Column(
        children: <Widget>[
          Text(
            "Sandeep Patel",
            style: Theme.of(context).textTheme.display1
                .copyWith(color: Colors.white),
          ),
          Expanded(child: Container()),
          Text("Email: s.patel@us.com",
              style: Theme.of(context)].textTheme.body2
                  .copyWith(color: Colors.white)),
          Text("Phone: +1 (555) 786-3512",
              style: Theme.of(context).textTheme.body2
                  .copyWith(color: Colors.white)),
        ],
      ),
    ],
  ),
),
```

In the Stack, we placed an image first. Then on top of that, we added a Column with text elements. Since the Column was added after the image, it appears in front of the image.

Positioned widget

In our preceding example, the texts laid out decently because a Column centers its children and the Expanded pushed the Texts to the top and bottom. But if we just had everything directly in the Stack, it would look like Figure 8-13.

Figure 8-13. *Without a Positioned widget everything bunches up in the upper left*

When you use a Stack, every widget inside it will try to stay in the top-left corner. We can place those inner widgets in a Stack anywhere we want by wrapping them in a Positioned widget.[2]

```
Card(
  child: Stack(
    children: <Widget>[
      Image.asset("6.jpg"),
      Positioned(
        top: 10, left: 10,
        child: Text("Sandeep Patel",
```

---

[2]There are other techniques to position inside of a Stack such as Container, Align, and Padding. But Position works great with Stack.

```
          style: Theme.of(context).textTheme.display1
              .copyWith(color: Colors.white),
        ),
      ),
      Positioned(
        bottom: 30, right: 10,
        child: Text("Email: s.patel@us.com",
            style: Theme.of(context).textTheme.body2
                .copyWith(color: Colors.white)),
      ),
      Positioned(
        bottom: 10, right: 10,
        child: Text("Phone: +1 (555) 786-3512",
            style: Theme.of(context).textTheme.body2
                .copyWith(color: Colors.white)),
      ),
      Positioned(
        bottom: 0, left: 0, height: 100, width: 100,
        child: FlutterLogo(),
      )
    ],
  ),
),
```

We threw in a FlutterLogo for good measure. It now looks like
Figure 8-14. Much nicer!

Figure 8-14. *Much nicer looking with a Positioned widget*

The Positioned widget makes its child a fixed distance from one of the four corners by specifying the top, bottom, left, and/or right positions.

Card widget

You may have noticed that we used a Card widget in our preceding example. A Card feels like the right thing to do in this situation, but it is by no means required.

A Flutter Card widget was created to implement the Material Design look and feel, having properties like color for the background color, elevation for a drop shadow size, borderOnForeground for the border, and margin for spacing around it. Granted, all of those could also be accomplished with a Container. But if you want to do it with a standard look and feel, a Card makes it easy:

```
Card(
  elevation: 20.0,
  child: Text("This is text in a card",
          style: Theme.of(context).textTheme.display3),
),
```

Themes

I don't know about you, but I love it when an app is well-planned, thought out, and designed beforehand. If it isn't, you can end up with this crazy quilt of colors and fonts with an unpredictable, uneven use of italics, bolding, and underlines. In short, you don't want to recreate http://lingscars.com.

A consistent use of styling creates a pleasant app that exudes quality. And a great way of staying consistent is simply to stick to a Theme.

A Theme in Flutter is a grouping of styles in logically-defined groups that can be applied together.

This way, not only does your app have a consistent look and feel throughout, but you can easily change the theme in one (1!) place, MaterialApp, and it propagates to all children:

```
class MyApp extends StatelessWidget {
  @override
  Widget build(BuildContext context) {
    return MaterialApp(
      title: 'Ch 8 - Styling Text',
      theme: ThemeData(primarySwatch: Colors.yellow),
      home: HomeWidget(),
    );
  }
}
```

If you do nothing else with themes, you're going to want to set the primarySwatch color. In doing so, you're actually setting all of the other colors. By setting primarySwatch, these are all automatically set also:

accentColor	backgroundColor	bottomAppBarColor
buttonColor	canvasColor	cardColor
colorScheme	cursorColor	dialogBackgroundColor
disabledColor	dividerColor	errorColor
highlightColor	hintColor	indicatorColor
primaryColor	primaryColorDark	primaryColorLight
scaffoldBackgroundColor	secondaryHeaderColor	selectedRowColor
splashColor	textSelectionColor	textSelectionHandleColor
toggleableActiveColor	unselectedWidgetColor	

This is extremely efficient. One line of code sets all of these other things to decent values. Of course if you have special requirements that call for one of these colors to change (i.e., your users are scared of the color red), then by all means change whatever you need. But you're generally going to want to use the defaults because each color is engineered to look good as a set alongside the primaryColor and all of the others.

There are lots of settings besides color in your Theme, things like size of tick marks in a slider, what kind of animations happen when navigating from scene to scene, whether modal dialogs have sharp or rounded corners, and so on. Just like with colors, feel free to change them if your app calls for it, but it is awesome that we aren't forced to deal with these minutiae and can focus on building a cool app.

Explore all of the properties in your Theme here: https://docs. flutter.io/flutter/material/ThemeData-class.html. It will take a while. There's a ton of options there. I'm just grateful that instead of having to manage them all, we can just set primarySwatch and be done with it!

You'll notice in that list that there's a textTheme, an appBarTheme, an InputDecorationTheme, a sliderTheme, and many more. Let's talk about these groupings for a second. Many *types* of thing in your app have a default theme which collects style properties for that type. When you add a widget of that type, it automatically gets the theme properties by default.

Applying theme properties

Remember, you don't have to do anything in order to use the themes on almost every widget in your app. Nothing. In fact, that's the whole idea of setting a Theme and some of the underlying properties; your app just absorbs them when they're rendered. The theme becomes their default look and feel.

But what if you want to overtly apply a theme? For instance, you have a Text widget at the top of a scene and you want it to function as a page heading. Or maybe below that somewhere you want a second-level heading. Perhaps a sub-heading somewhere. How do you tell these special Text widgets that they are supposed to be drawn in a special way? Remember the style property?

Text widgets have a style property that takes a TextStyle object. But you can access well-known text styles from the theme like so:

```
Text('title', style: Theme.of(context).textTheme.title),
Text('subtitle', style: Theme.of(context).textTheme.subtitle),
Text('headline', style: Theme.of(context).textTheme.headline),
Text('subhead', style: Theme.of(context).textTheme.subhead),
```

You have the Material textThemes in Table 8-1 to choose from.

Table 8-1. *Material theme text styles*

Text theme name	Description
body1	Most of the text you see. This will be the default style if you don't explicitly apply one
body2	Slightly thicker body text
button	The default font on buttons, typically all caps and spread out a bit
caption	For photo captions
display1	The smallest headline (aka headline4)
display2	The 3rd biggest headline (aka headline3)
display3	The 2nd biggest headline (aka headline2)
display4	The biggest headline (aka headline1)
headline	Your go-to style for headlines (aka headline5)
subhead	For subheadings. Usually right below a heading.
title	(aka headline6)
subtitle	For sub-subheadings. Usually right below a title
overline	Rarely used. For introducing a headline

Figure 8-15 shows what they all look like.

Figure 8-15. *How the Material text styles look on a device*

Tip   When you want to apply a style from a theme but want to change a few properties, use copyWith(). Here's an example:

```
Text('Foo', style:
    Theme.of(context).textTheme.body2.copyWith(color:Colors.red),
),
```

You're reaching up into a current style and making a copy of it but altering one or two properties for this instance. This allows you to use your slightly customized style while leaving the original unaltered.

Conclusion

So you can see that the options for styling things in Flutter are near infinite. Flutter styling resembles what you may have seen in CSS, but is by no means the same. First, it is more verbose. And second, it doesn't inherit. Some people may resent these characteristics, but others will like the cleanness that it creates.

Regardless of how you feel about that, you've got to be impressed with the styling options that Flutter provides, especially when you think about how they're organized in Themes so we can present a consistent, professional look and feel throughout our app.

Now, for the moment you've all been waiting for ... let's learn how to handle Stateful widgets!

CHAPTER 9

Managing State

We kind of telegraphed this topic since the first chapter because we've been writing classes that extend a StatelessWidget. Now if Flutter has a State*less*Widget, then you'd think it also has a State*ful*Widget. And you'd be right.

But what exactly is a StatefulWidget? How does it differ from a stateless one? When do we choose one vs. the other? What is the structure of a StatefulWidget? Are there rules for using one? If the data changes, how do you re-render it? Good questions, right? Well, be patient young Jedi and we'll answer all of those and more in this chapter.

What is state?

> *State is widget data whose change requires a re-render.*
>
> —Rap Payne ;-)

StatelessWidgets might have data, but that data either doesn't change or doesn't change how the screen looks while the widget is alive. Sure, it may change when Flutter destroys and recreates the widget, but that doesn't count. To be state, it must change while the widget is active, and that change requires a re-render in order to stay current.

© Rap Payne 2019
R. Payne, *Beginning App Development with Flutter*,
https://doi.org/10.1007/978-1-4842-5181-2_9

Flutter gives us certain widgets that are stateful out of the box

- AppBar
- BottomNavigationBar
- Checkbox
- DefaultTabController
- Dismissible
- DrawerController
- DropdownButton
- EditableText
- Form
- FormField
- GlowingOverscrollIndicator
- Image
- InputDecorator
- MonthPicker
- Navigator
- ProgressIndicator
- Radio
- RefreshIndicator
- Scaffold
- Scrollbar
- Slider
- Switch
- TextField
- YearPicker

... and many more. These all have internal data that must be maintained and monitored so that as the data changes, we re-render the widget to reflect the said change.

Let's take a simple example: a TextField widget. Yes, we're talking about the built-in widget that's kind of like a textbox on the Web; the user can type characters into it. You realize of course that as the user types, the widget is keeping track of and displaying the stuff that they're typing. That, my friend, is state.

That's great and all, but how do we write our own StatefulWidgets? Read on!

What goes in a StatefulWidget?

Here's the shape of a StatefulWidget:

```
class Foo extends StatefulWidget {
  @override
  _FooState createState() => _FooState();
}
class _FooState extends State<Foo> {
  //Private variables here are considered the 'state'
  @override
  Widget build(BuildContext context) {
    return someWidget;
  }
}
```

A stateful widget looks pretty complex, but once you get used to its structure, it becomes second nature. We traditionally write it in one Dart file, but it always consists of two classes: the widget class and a state class.

The widget class inherits from StatefulWidget and is public because it is the thing that will be placed in other widgets.

The state class is always private because the current widget is the only thing that will ever see this class. The state class is responsible to ...

1. Define and maintain the state data.

2. Define the build() method – It knows how to draw the widget on screen.

3. Define any callback functions needed for data gathering or event handling.

What does that leave for the widget class? Not much. The widget class just kind of gets out of the way.

So then why separate them? There are two reasons. First, the single responsibility principle[1] (the SRP) suggests that we should have one thing responsible for drawing the widget and another thing responsible for dealing with data. That's just good software design. Other frameworks suggest that you separate UI from state management, but most don't enforce it. Flutter does.

Second is performance. Redrawing takes time. Recalculating state takes time. When we separate them like this, we are giving the processor a chance to handle these two things independently. Sometimes a redraw doesn't need to happen just because state changes. So we save the cycles of redrawing.

Also, when we redraw, Flutter creates and draws a whole new widget. The old widget in memory is no longer needed so it is dereferenced and eventually garbage collected. That's awesome but state is still needed. If Flutter retains that old state object, it can be reused instead of being garbage collected and recreated. By separating these objects, Flutter decouples them so they can each be handled in its own most efficient way. It's a brilliant design!

The most important rule about state!

When you change any state value, you should do it ...

1. In the state class

2. Inside a function call to setState():

```
setState(() {
  // Make all changes to state variables here...
  _value = 42; // <-- ... Like this
});
```

---

[1]https://en.wikipedia.org/wiki/Single_responsibility_principle

setState() takes a function which is run ... uh ... soon. The Flutter subsystem batches changes and runs them all at a time that it decides is optimal. This is extremely efficient because, among other reasons, it will reduce the number of screen redraws.

setState() not only sets the variables in the most efficient and controlled way, but it always forces a re-render of this widget to occur. It invokes build() behind the scenes. The end result: When you change a value, the widget redraws itself and your user sees the new version. Note that if this widget has subwidgets inside of it (aka *inner* widgets), they'll be in the build() method, so a call to setState() actually redraws **everything** in this widget including all of its subtrees.

If this causes you to panic for a second, please remember that Flutter uses a virtual widget tree, so even though we are telling it to draw everything, it is smart enough to know what parts of the screen don't need a refresh and it only technically redraws those parts that do need it. It is superefficient!

Passing state <u>down</u>

Okay, you got me. Technically, you can't pass state from a host widget into an inner widget because state only exists *within* a widget. But we definitely want to pass data down. That data may be stateful data in the host widget, and it may be moved to state in the inner widget.

But this is nothing new. We did it with stateless widgets. As a reminder, you simply declare class-scoped final variables and supply their initial values in constructor parameters.

But how is the passed value visible in the State class? Flutter provides us an object called widget which represents the StatefulWidget. In other words, if there is a variable called "x" in the StatefulWidget, it is visible in the State class as "widget.x":

```
class Foo extends StatefulWidget {
  final String passedIn;
  // Value passed in from its host
  ColorValueChanger({Key key, this.passedIn}) : super(key: key);
  _FooState createState() => new _FooState();
}
class _FooState extends State<Foo> {
  @override
  Widget build(BuildContext context) {
    return Text(widget.passedIn,);
  }
}
```

Now that we know how to pass data down from host widget to inner widget, let's go the other way and see how to pass data back up from the inner widget to the host.

Lifting state back up

And you got me again. You can't pass state. But it gets worse. With Flutter, you can't pass anything *up*.

Flutter has one-way data flow. Period. Data can only flow down from a host widget to an inner widget. We've been doing this for, what, about 200 pages now? But sometimes we need data to flow from an inner back up to a host.

For instance, let's say we have a Login.dart widget with username/password textfields and a submit button. We'd place this Login in other widgets provided that the user is not already logged in. The business logic to log in must be in the Login widget itself. But when they successfully log in, we really need to let the host widget – or even all widgets – know they are now authenticated. The token needs to be passed back up. But how do we do that when we can't pass data (state) up to a host?

Here's the trick. Don't pass the data *up*. Pass the handler method *down*! In Dart (as in JavaScript), functions are first-class objects. This means that their references can be passed around like data. This also means that you can pass a function from a host widget down into inner widgets. Now that the inner widget has a handle to this function, it can call it as if it were its own. But of course when the inner widget calls it, if it passes a value into that function, the value is seen in the host where the function is defined.

This technique is called *lifting the state up* (Figure 9-1).

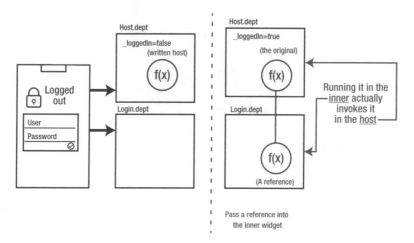

Figure 9-1. *Lifting state up*

An example of state management

We should probably look at some code to solidify these concepts. Let's say we have an app that allows its user to create a color by adjusting red, green, and blue values on three sliders. These will mix the colors and show it in a bigger circle (Figure 9-2).

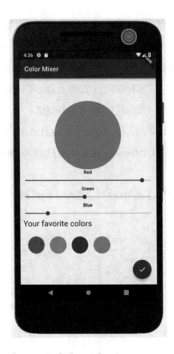

Figure 9-2. *An example stateful widget*

Clearly the big circle needs to redraw as data changes so we must have state. While we technically could have all of this in one big widget called ColorMixer, we've learned in this book to decompose large widgets into smaller, more specialized ones. Let's extract the ColorCircle and use it for the big circle and also for the favorite colors at the bottom. And since we've got three sliders with labels, all doing the same thing we should probably extract that also into a ColorValueChanger. So how about the layout in Figure 9-3?

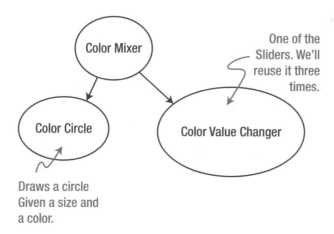

Figure 9-3. *How we might lay out the widget tree*

The ColorMixer must be stateful:

```
import 'package:flutter/material.dart';
import 'ColorCircle.dart';
import 'ColorValueChanger.dart';
// The stateful widget
class ColorMixer extends StatefulWidget {
 ColorMixer({Key key}) : super(key: key);
 _ColorMixerState createState() => _ColorMixerState();
}
// The state object
class _ColorMixerState extends State<ColorMixer> {
 // These three variables are the 'state' of the widget
 int _red = 0;
 int _blue = 0;
 int _green = 0;
```

```
@override
Widget build(BuildContext context) {
  return Container(
    child: Column(
      children: <Widget>[
        // This widget uses the variables (aka state)
        ColorCircle(color: Color.fromRGBO(_red, _green, _blue, 1),
                  radius: 200,),
        // These three pass the _setColor function down so that the
        // state *here* can be changed at lower levels. This is
        // called "lifting state up".
        ColorValueChanger(property: "Red", value:_red,
                        onChanged: _setColor),
        ColorValueChanger(property: "Green", value:_green,
                        onChanged: _setColor),
        ColorValueChanger(property: "Blue", value:_blue,
                        onChanged: _setColor),
      ],
    ),
  );
}
void _setColor(String property, int value) {
  setState(() {
    _red = (property == "Red") ? value : _red;
    _green = (property == "Green") ? value : _green;
    _blue = (property == "Blue") ? value : _blue;
  });
}
}
```

Note that we're passing 100% of what ColorCircle needs into it and it doesn't change throughout the life of ColorCircle. If ColorMixer's state changes, we simply call setState(), thereby re-rendering it … including ColorCircle. Thus, ColorCircle can be stateless.

In the same way, we pass an initial value into each ColorValueChanger, and we pass a reference to the _setColor method. Remember, passing a function down makes it available in the inner widget and therefore executable. Although the inner widget executes it, the function actually exists in the host widget!

Here's how it would look in the inner ColorValueChanger widget:

```
@override
Widget build(BuildContext context) {
  return Container(
    child: Column(
      children: <Widget>[
        Text(property),
        Slider(
          min: 0,
          max: 255,
          value: _value.toDouble(),
          label: property,
          onChanged: _onChanged,
        ),
      ],
    ),
  );
}
_onChanged(double value) {
  setState(() => _value = value.round());
  onChanged(property, value.round());  // Lifting state up
}
```

When should we use state?

But you know what? The very best way to avoid complex state is to avoid having state at all. Just about every expert agrees that if you can avoid state altogether, do. But it can be confusing as to when you need state and when you don't.

For example, the label on our color picker is data within the component. Should that be state? No, of course not; it doesn't change. How about a loop counter on a for loop? Nope; it never affects anything in the build() method, so it doesn't need to be put in a setState(). See? State can sometimes be simplified or eliminated.

Figure 9-4 provides a summary of how to decide.

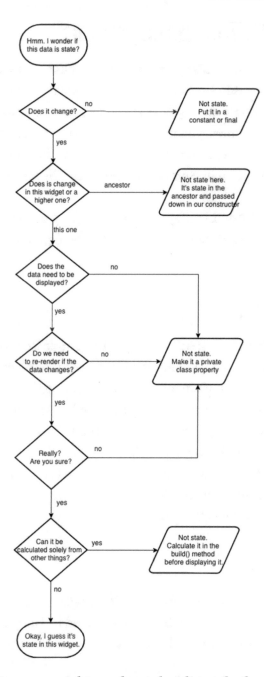

Figure 9-4. *How you might go about deciding whether state should actually be used in a widget*

Advanced state management

What we've looked at in this chapter would work as advertised even when the widget tree gets infinitely deep. But please realize that as your app gets bigger and bigger, state management become more and more complex. When it gets too complex, you may be better served by using a more advanced state management pattern. These patterns are not always easy to learn, but at some point in your app's growth, they become worth the effort to master.

We wanted to keep this chapter digestible so we can't go into details on all of these technologies, but we also didn't want to pretend the problem doesn't exist.

InheritedWidget

This is a relatively simple solution, maybe too simple for most needs. InheritedWidget[2] is a built-in Flutter widget. Essentially it creates a small set of global variables that are made available in a controlled way to all descendants in its tree. Several of the other methods (ScopedModel, Provider, Redux) are wrappers around InheritedWidget.

Pros: No library to install or keep track of.

Cons: There is some duplication between the InheritedWidget and the underlying StatefulWidget. That's a shame. Also the entire subtree is re-rendered when any data changes.

BLoC

BLoC is an acronym for Business Logic Component, and it's less of a solution than a design pattern. BLoC was created by Google so naturally; it was embraced by the Flutter community.

---

[2]https://docs.flutter.io/flutter/widgets/InheritedWidget-class.html

Pros: Lots of folks in the community can and will help you. It is a solid, well-vetted pattern.

Cons: You have to write everything yourself; it's neither built-in nor a library. It can be hard to know where to inject a BLoC.

ScopedModel

ScopedModel[3] is a library "shamelessly borrowed" from the Fuchsia[4] codebase by Brian Egan. (Hey, these are Brian's words, not mine! He's a humble guy.) ScopedModel creates data models with the ability to register listeners. Each model notifies its listeners when the data has changed so they can update. Clever design.

Pros: Does its job of separating presentation and data very well.

Cons: There is talk of ScopedModel being combined with Google's flutter_provide[5] which seems to be a more modern and simpler approach to state management.

Hooks

An implementation of React hooks by Rémi Rousselet of Paris called flutter_hooks.[6] You no longer use StatefulWidgets at all. Instead you inherit from a HookWidget which is stateless (therefore simpler) but allows you to create and access custom functions that read and write state values. It even comes with some pre-baked hooks that you don't have to write.

Pros: Greatly simplifies your formerly stateless widgets.

Cons: Learning curve. It isn't obvious how they work and the rules for use unless you're already familiar with React hooks.

---

[3]https://pub.dartlang.org/packages/scoped_model
[4]https://fuchsia.googlesource.com/
[5]https://pub.dartlang.org/packages/provide
[6]https://pub.dartlang.org/documentation/flutter_hooks

Provider

At the time of this writing, there's some confusion between Provider,[7] also written by Rémi Rousselet, and a similarly named one written by Filip Hracek and the good folks at Google. Filip freely admits that Rémi's package "is more feature-ful"[8] (sic).

Pros: A very robust and capable package that is comparatively simple to use. In the near future, I expect this to become the go-to state management library for developers who don't already have a leaning toward Redux and/or hooks because of prior experience with the React ecosystem.

Cons: Not (yet) as popular as some of the others.

Note that there is a lot of confusion between this package and flutter-provide created by Google because of the naming. The latter one, taken from the Fuchsia codebase and open-sourced, may be combined with ScopedModel and deprecated.

Redux

Like a few others on this list, Redux is a library borrowed from other technologies and ported to Dart. Redux has a deep history coming from the world of React via Facebook. There are several implementations, but the most popular is here: flutter_redux.[9] Also written by the prolific Brian Egan.

Cons: Very steep learning curve.

Pros: Very performant. Very scalable. Many React developers already know Redux.js. The learning curve flattens significantly for them.

---

[7]https://pub.dartlang.org/packages/provider
[8]https://github.com/google/flutter-provide/issues/3
[9]https://pub.dartlang.org/packages/flutter_redux

Whoa! That's a lot of packages!

Confused yet? I don't blame you. These packages all solve the same problem in different ways, some similarly and others using wildly different strategies. No one has any expectations that you'll have anything more than an awareness that there are tools out there. When you hear someone say something like "Our state is getting messy. Maybe we should take a look at BLoC or ScopedModel," you'll at least know that type of thing they're talking about. Then you can dig into the technologies to see which you might want to use.

Conclusion

There are clear times when a widget needs to maintain its own status via the data that is contained within it. When we do, we call this *state* and we call the widget a stateful widget. Stateful widgets are by their nature more complex than stateless widgets so we try to avoid them if we can. Additionally the more stateful widgets we have, the more state needs to be passed around between the widgets. This can get very complex very quickly so we look to tools and techniques like BLoC, Redux, ScopedModel, and Provider to tame state.

Fortunately, this is as complex as fundamental Flutter gets. Not so bad after all. Since we've covered everything that is needed to create a Flutter app, this ends the section. In the remainder of the book, let's turn to additional, perhaps optional topics that will help you to create real-world Flutter apps!

PART III

Above and Beyond

CHAPTER 10

Your Flutter App Can Work with Files

At this point in our journey, you've learned how to create a Flutter app and precisely control how it looks and lays out in any orientation and on any device. That's pretty cool! You know how to have it maintain data with Form fields. But how do we get it to save that data? How do we get it to read that data in the first place?

Your app's data can only come from two places: from within the device itself or by exchanging data with an external server. We'll deal with external servers in the next chapter. In this chapter, let's learn to read and write data from on-device storage options. But in order to get there by the end of the chapter, we have to master certain prerequisite knowledge like working with JSON and handling asynchronous activities. So here will be our plan for the chapter:

- Including libraries in your Flutter app

- Bundling files in your app

- Futures, async, and await

- Reading/writing a local file

- Converting JSON

- Saving user preferences

© Rap Payne 2019
R. Payne, *Beginning App Development with Flutter*,
https://doi.org/10.1007/978-1-4842-5181-2_10

Including libraries in your Flutter app

Many talented developers have written some awesome tools that you and I can use in our Flutter apps. These are usually referred to as libraries, and all we have to do is (1) find one that we like, (2) add it to our pubspec.yaml file, (3) import it in a dart file, and (4) use it in our code.

Finding a library

Frankly, this is the hardest part because there's no single place to search. As lame as it sounds, your best bet is to Google it. Later in this chapter, we'll be reading and writing a file so let's use that as an example. If you Google for "Flutter read file," every one of the top five results recommends using a library called path_provider. So we Google for "Flutter path_provider" and we end up at `https://pub.dev/packages/path_provider`, as shown in Figure 10-1.

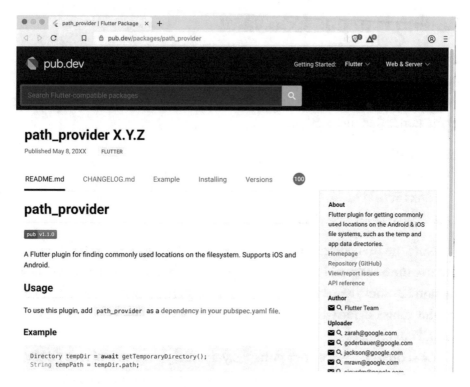

Figure 10-1. *path_provider 1.3.0 home page*

As you can see, the page gives us a version number (which we've anonymized to X.Y.Z in the preceding screenshot), how to use the library, and code samples plus more.

Adding it to pubspec.yaml

The Usage section tells you what you need to know to use it. There is no download button and no installation. In fact, all you have to do for nearly every Flutter/dart library is to just edit the pubspec.yaml file and add a line to the dependencies section:

```
dependencies:
  flutter:
    sdk: flutter
  path_provider: ^X.Y.Z
```

Note the preceding carat (^). That says to the developer tools, "You can use the latest version of the library as long as you don't go above major version X." Some experienced Flutter developers think that it is risky to let the dev tools decide which version of the library to use so they omit the carat. Your choice.

As soon as you save your pubspec.yaml file, your dev tools may detect the new library and go get it for you. If not, just run flutter pub get.

```
$ flutter pub get
Running "flutter pub get" in myProject...        0.7s
$
```

Now that it is downloaded, you can begin using it.

Importing the library

Open any source code file where you'll need the functionality of this library and add an import statement to the top:

```
import 'package:flutter/material.dart';
import 'package:path_provider/path_provider.dart';
```

You'll know what to import by reading the library's documentation. See? Easy.

Using the library

How to use it depends heavily on the library and of course no two are alike. The instructions and examples are found in the documentation again. And the documentation for path_provider tells us to call a method called getTemporaryDirectory() or getApplicationDocumentsDirectory() like this:

```
Directory documents = await getApplicationDocumentsDirectory();
File file = File('${documents.path}/$_filename');
```

"But wait," you say, "What is this await thing?" Let's talk about that next.

Futures, async, and await

Flutter is written using Dart, and Dart is a single-threaded language. This means that a Flutter app can only do one thing at a time, but it does not mean that Flutter apps are forced to wait for slower processes.

Flutter apps use an event loop. This should come as no surprise since Android has a main looper and iOS has a run loop (aka main loop). Heck, even JavaScript devs are unimpressed since JavaScript itself has a … wait for it … event loop. Yes, all the cool kids are using an event loop these days.

An event loop is a background infinite loop which periodically wakes up and looks in the event queue for any tasks that need to run. If any exist, the event loops put them onto the run stack if and only if the CPU is idle.

As your app is running instructions, they run serially – one after another. If an instruction is encountered that may potentially block the main thread waiting on some resource, it is started and the "wait" part is put on a separate queue.

Why would it wait?

Certain things are slow compared to the CPU. Reading from a file is slow. Writing to a file is even slower. Communicating via Ajax? Forget about it. If we kept the waiting activity on the main thread, it would block all other commands. What a waste!

The way this is handled in JavaScript, iOS, Android, and now Dart is this:

1. An activity that is well-known to be slow is started up as normal.

2. The moment it begins waiting for something – disk, HTTP request, whatever – it is moved away from the CPU.

3. A listener of sorts is created. It monitors the activity and raises an alert when it is finished waiting.

4. The reference to that listener is returned to the main thread. This reference object is known as a Future.

5. The main thread continues chugging along its merry way.

6. When the waiting activity is finally resolved, the event loop sees it and runs an associated method (aka. a callback function) on the main thread to handle finishing up the slow event.

All you do is write the code to create the future and to handle futures that are returned from other methods:

```
// Say goReadAFile() is slow and returns a Future
Future myFuture = goReadAFile();
```

In Dart you have the ability to specify the type of thing that Future will give you eventually:

Type of future	When it's ready, I'll have a ...
Future<String>	... string
Future<Foo>	... Foo
Future<Map<String, dynamic>>	... Map whose keys are Strings and whose values are dynamic

When we have that Future object, you may not have the data, but you definitely have a promise to get that data in the Future. (See what they did there?)

How do we get the data from a Future?

You tell the Future what to do once the data is ready. Basically, you're responding to a "Yo, the data is ready" event and telling the Future what to do by registering a function.

```
myFuture.then(myCallback);
```

The .then() function is how you register that callback function. The callback should be written to handle the promised data. For example, if we have a Future<Foo>, then our callback should have this signature:

```
void myCallback(Foo theIncomingData) {
 doSomethingWith(theIncomingData);
}
```

So if the Future will return a Person, your callback should receive a Person. If the Future promises a String, your callback should receive a String. And so forth.

Your callbacks should always return void because there's no way that the .then function can receive a returned value. This makes a ton of sense when you think about it because remember that it is no longer running within the main thread of your app so it has no way of merging back in. So how do you get a value from the callback? Several methods, but the most understandable is that you use a variable that is defined outside the callback:

```
class FooState extends State<FooComponent> {
  String _firstName;  // <-- A variable known by the whole class
  Widget build(BuildContext context) {
    // return a widget
  }
  void _myCallback(String someVar) {
    _firstName = someVar;  // <-- Getting a value OUT of an
                                        async callback

  }
}
```

Tacking a .then() onto your Future object can occasionally muddy up your code. If you prefer, you can clean it up a bit with *await*.

await

There's another way to get the data which is more straightforward to read. Instead of using .then(), you can *await* the data.

```
Foo theIncomingData = await somethingThatReturnsAFuture();
```

Awaiting pauses the running code to ... well ... wait for the Future to resolve before it moves on to the next line. In the preceding example, the "Foo" that you're awaiting is returned and put into theIncomingData. Simple.

Or maybe it isn't that simple...

214

async

Like it or not, when you use await inside a function, that function is now in danger of blocking the main thread, so it must be marked as async. For example, this function

```
Bar someFunction() {
  Foo theIncomingData = someFunction();
  return new Bar();
}
```

becomes this when we await

```
Future<Bar> someFunction() async {
  Foo theIncomingData = await somethingThatReturnsAFuture();
  return new Bar();
}
```

Note that when we added an await on that second line, we must mark the function itself with async. The subtle thing is that when it is marked as async, anything returned from that function is immediately wrapped in a Future unless it is already one.

Are you sitting down? Check this out: whenever you choose to await a future, the function must be marked as async, and therefore all who call it must be awaited and they must be marked as async and so on. Eventually you get to a high enough spot in the call chain that you're not in a function so you don't have to mark it as async.

Maybe I spoke too soon when I said this is simpler.

Hint   The Flutter build() method cannot be async, but events like onPress can. So try to steer your async activities into events to solve this recursive async-await-async-await thing.

Here are your Futures takeaways:

1. Futures allow your Dart code to be asynchronous
   – it can handle slow-running processes in a separate
   thread (kind of).

2. You can handle the callbacks of those things with
   either a .then(callback) or by awaiting them.

3. If you await in a function, that function must be
   marked as async.

If you'd like to do some more reading on Futures, here's a thorough
coverage from the Dart team: `www.dartlang.org/tutorials/language/
futures`.

Including a file with your app

The file you're trying to read must exist (duh). Maybe we should just
manually create one.

It isn't uncommon at all for developers to package up a flat file that
should be installed along with your app. It is great for initializations
of larger amounts of data – kind of like a mini database. It should look
familiar because this is the same technique we used to bundle images
with our app. All you'll do is create the file in your IDE and reference it in
pubspec.yaml.

There are a dozen ways to add the file to your project. Use a command
prompt, right-click and choose "new" in your IDE, drag and drop in file
explorer, and so on. But in the end, it should be visible in your IDE.

It is common but not required to create it in a folder called assets
(Figure 10-2).

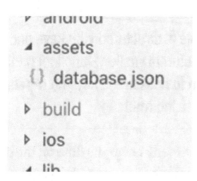

Figure 10-2. *"assets" folder*

But even though it exists, the app is unaware of a file until we flag it in pubspec.yaml. Put it in the assets section of pubspec.yaml and it will be included with the .ipa/.apk for installation on devices:

```
# To add assets to your app, add an assets section, like this:
assets:
  - assets/database.json
```

To read that file, you'll use rootBundle.loadString() like this:

```
try {
  String data = await rootBundle.loadString('assets/db.json');
  debugPrint(data);
} catch (e) {
  print('Error: $e');
  rethrow;
}
```

rootBundle is part of services.dart, so make sure you import it.

```
import 'package:flutter/services.dart';
```

Tip   If the assets file is structured with keys and values, the rootBundle.loadStructuredData(key, function) method may be a better choice. It allows you to pass in the key you're reading and a function to process the data being read.

Since this data is written at compile time on the development machine, it can't be changed. But we can create a file in our app's documents folder that can be read and written. Let's look at that next.

Writing a file

Sometimes our users want to save values from one run to another. And we can do that in a local file, one that exists on their device. To create a file, you can simply write to it with myFile.writeAsString(theString). But our app can't just write to any location on the device. We have to get a reference to a writeable directory which is exactly what the path_provider library does. Remember that it has a method called getApplicationDocumentsDirectory() which returns a Future<Directory>. So if we await that call, we can get a directory and create a file in it:

```
// Get the documents directory
Directory documents = await getApplicationDocumentsDirectory();
// Write the file
try {
  File file = File('${documents.path}/$_filename');
  await file.writeAsString(_someText);
} catch (e) {
  _message = 'Error: $e';
}
```

Note   The Directory and File types are available in Dart's io library.
Don't forget to import it:

```
import 'dart:io';
```

And reading it!

Reading any file is even simpler. We just use File.readAsString():

```
File file = File('${documents.path}/$_filename');
file.readAsString().then((String text) {
  setState(() {
    _text = text;
    _message = '$_filename has this text inside it: "$_text"';
  });
}).catchError((e) {
  setState(() {
    _errorStatus = true;
    _message = 'Error: $e';
  });
});
```

Note   We wanted to use the .then() method of the future here
instead of await because the build() method can't be marked as
async. The .then() allows you to handle the future without the need
for async. Fortunately the File object also has a readAsStringSync()
method which is a blocking call and returns the text directly instead
of a Future.

```
try {
  File file = File('${documents.path}/$_filename');
  _text = file.readAsStringSync();
  // Modal success
  _message = '$_filename has this text inside it: "$_text"';
} catch (e) {
  _errorStatus = true;
  _message = 'Error: $e';
}
```

Using JSON

When we write files, we're taking something in our app's memory and saving it. Sure, sometimes what we write is just a single value, but very often it is an object or many objects. Let's say we had a list of persons. Maybe the first person in the list is Phoebe Buffay and the second is Rachel Green. If we're going to save this list in a file, we'd have to designate it as a list and specify the properties and values of each person. There are unlimited ways of doing that, but the most popular one is JSON format:

```
{
  "people": [
    {
      "id": "7b5fa0b0-9760-11e9-805d-099f65ed4f55",
      "firstName": "Phoebe",
      "lastName": "Buffay",
      "occupation": "Massage Therapist"
    },
    {
      "id": "110ec58a-a0f2-4ac4-8393-c866d813b8d1",
      "firstName": "Rachel",
```

```
      "lastName": "Green",
      "occupation": "Coffee Waitress"
    }
  ]
}
```

Taking data in our app's memory and putting it in that format is called *serializing* the data. Going the other direction, reading data in JSON format, unwrapping it, and loading it into our app's memory is called *deserialization*.

Dart has a built-in library called dart:convert with methods for serializing and deserializing called json.encode() and json.decode(), respectively.

Writing your app's memory to JSON

Say your app has an object that you want to store or transmit. To put that data in JSON format, use json.encode(someMap):

```
Map<String, dynamic> jsonMap = {
  "id": _person.id,
  "firstName": _person.firstName,
  "lastName": _person.lastName,
  "occupation": _person.occupation,
};
try {
  String jsonString = json.encode(jsonMap)
  await file.writeAsString(jsonString);
} catch (e) {
  print("Problem saving! Error: $e");
}
```

> **Note**   A Dart Map is kind of like a JavaScript object; a set of key/
> value pairs, usually dynamically typed. To get a value, you'd specify
> a key in square brackets like in the following example. If you want to
> serialize a strongly typed object, you can either convert it to a map
> (easier) or implement a method called toJson() which returns a Map
> (cleaner). toJson() is automatically invoked whenever json.encode is
> called on an object.

Reading JSON into your app's memory

Now let's say you've somehow gotten ahold of a string in JSON format and
you want to read that data into your app. How do you get that data out?
json.decode():

```
// jsonString contain serialized JSON data
Map<String, dynamic> personMap = json.decode(jsonString);
// "personMap" is now a Map whose keys are strings
print(personMap["firstName"]);
Person p = Person(
  id: personMap["id"],
  firstName: person ["firstName"],
  lastName: person ["lastName"],
  occupation: person ["occupation"]
);
```

> **Note**   jsonEncode() is shorthand for json.encode(). Similarly
> jsonDecode() is shorthand for json.decode(). It's a stylistic preference.
> Use whichever you prefer.

You may be thinking about using this technique to store a user's preferences. And sure, it'll totally work. But if you want to save values between runs of the app, there is a better way called *shared preferences*.

Shared preferences

Most apps will save data locally between runs, settings like authentication tokens, personal data, dark/light modes, sounds ... heck, anything that would be a user preference. On iOS these things are called NSUserDefaults. On Android, they are called SharedPreferences. And the Flutter team has given us a great library called shared_preferences[1] for reading and writing these values in a cross-platform way. Now that you know how to include libraries, it'll be trivial for you to add shared_preferences to your pubspec. yaml file to include it in your project and app.

To use it, you'll need to instantiate a SharedPreferences object. But since we're dealing with reading from the file system, it needs to be handled as a deferred activity. Fortunately the library provides a static getInstance() method that returns a Future<SharedPreference>. I know all that sounds confusing, but just remember that getting a reference to the reader/writer is asynchronous. Handle it like this:

```
SharedPreferences prefs = await SharedPreferences.
getInstance();
```

See? That's not so bad. But do note that it has to be awaited.

---

[1]Read up on it at https://pub.dev/packages/shared_preferences

To write preferences

To save to shared preferences, use the set methods:

```
prefs
  ..setString('organizationName', organizationName)
  ..setBool('isReady', true)
  ..setDouble('percentComplete', 12.5)
  ..setInt('numberOfTries', tries)
  ..setStringList('validValues', ['started','finished',
                                 'in process', 'approved']);
```

Each of these will save to the right incarnation of device-dependent user preferences and return back a Future<bool>, the bool resolving to true if it was successful and false if not. It is not a problem to ignore this value if you want. Many developers do when they're ignoring the extremely rare exception.

To read preferences

If writing is with *set* methods, then you'd assume reading is *get* methods and you'd be correct:

```
String organizationName = prefs.getString('organizationName');
bool isReady = prefs.getBool('isReady');
double percentComplete = prefs.getDouble('percentComplete');
int numberOfTries = prefs.getInt('numberOfTries');
List<String> validValues = prefs.getStringList('validValues');
```

Conclusion

As we said at the top of the chapter, we're building up to exchanging data with a server, which is a very complex topic. But what makes it complex is that there are so many technologies and techniques involved: third-party libraries, JSON serialization and deserialization, Futures, and asynchronous reading and writing. But because we've handled those topics in this chapter, what's left won't be so daunting.

Ready to learn about Ajax? Let's do it!

CHAPTER 11

Making RESTful API Calls with HTTP

Now we know how to create a Flutter app, use external libraries and asynchronously read and write data in JSON format. That actually puts us in a great position to go just one small step forward and exchange data with an API server, something that is absolutely essential if we are going to write real-world apps. Here's what we need to know:

- What is an API call anyway?

- Making an HTTP GET or DELETE request.

- Making an HTTP POST, PUT, or PATCH request.

- Handling the response in the simplest way.

- Cleaner handling with FutureBuilder and StreamBuilder.

- Cleaner handling with strongly typed objects.

That'll be our plan for this chapter. That, and getting in some hands-on practice with a web site that allows HTTP updates. And to make sure everyone is on the same page (pun definitely intended), we should probably start with what exactly an API is. Feel free to skim it or skip altogether if you're already familiar.

© Rap Payne 2019
R. Payne, *Beginning App Development with Flutter*,
https://doi.org/10.1007/978-1-4842-5181-2_11

What is an *API* call?

Your app already has the ability to read from a tiny, localized database. But it cannot read from one that is located *elsewhere*. In other words, you can't just connect to the Google database and read or write records. Can't be done, not even if you have database credentials. I mean, think about the security implications if everyone could connect from anywhere and directly modify Google data. So what developers do instead is create and run a server-side program to read and write in a controlled way and expose that program on the Internet at a particular address with a particular protocol, usually https.

To read this server-side data, any user can make http requests after having sent their credentials in the form of username/password or better yet, a unique and secret key called an API key.

There's that term *API* again. It stands for Application Programming Interface. It means different things in different situations, but its default meaning has come to be any Internet address to which developers can send http requests for the purpose of reading and writing data. There are tons of publicly available APIs and many options for creating your own.

When an API responds, it returns with a stream of data that is almost always in JSON[1] format.

The flavors of API requests

Communication with API servers is done in one of just a few flavors (Table 11-1).

---

[1] Read up on JSON here: https://json.org

Table 11-1. *HTTP methods and descriptions*

HTTP method	Intent	Notes
GET	Reading records	Like a database read, merely asking for data from a server
DELETE	Deleting records	Delete the record pointed to by the supplied ID. No data is returned
POST	Inserting new records	Create a new record even if there's already a record like this one
PUT	Replacing existing records	Clobber the existing record with this one. Delete the old record completely and add this one in its place
PATCH	Updating existing records	Keep the old record in place but update its fields with the data from this request

HEAD, CONNECT, OPTIONS, TRACE – For other types of requests. Seldom used by typical apps. Read about them at `http://bit.ly/HTTPMethods` if you want.

It is rare for developers to use anything other than GET, POST, PUT, PATCH, and DELETE. They're all done in Flutter by using one Dart library which you'll get by importing http.dart.

First, you'll add the http package to the dependencies section of your pubspec.yaml. When you add and run "flutter pub get," the package will be downloaded from `https://pub.dev/packages/http`.

```
import 'package:http/http.dart';
```

This will expose the http class which has methods corresponding to each HTTP method. Now let's look at sending requests using this library.

Making an HTTP GET or DELETE request

We'll begin with GET and DELETE requests first because they are the simplest; they never have a body.[2] In fact, the only complexity is that HTTP requests are done asynchronously. They return a Future which you either need to handle with a .then() or await it. So maybe make your request like this:

```
String url = 'https://us.com/people/1234';
Response response = await get(url);
print(response.statusCode); // 200, we hope
Map<String, dynamic> person = json.decode(response.body);
print(person['first']);
print(person['last']);
print(person['imageUrl']);
print(person['email']);
```

or with a .then() like this:

```
get(url).then((Response res) {
  print(res.statusCode); // 200, we hope
  Map<String, dynamic> person = jsonDecode(res.body);
  print(person['first']);
  print(person['last']);
  print(person['imageUrl']);
  print(person['email']);
});
```

Delete requests are done in the same way. In fact, they are often simpler because they often have no response values. The DELETE

---

[2]This is hotly debated topic. While the HTTP spec is silent, RFC 2616 hints that a body is ignored in a DELETE request but doesn't explicitly forbid it. Some servers will ignore the body. Other servers will ignore the entire request. While others throw a 400 error. Either test it on your server or play it safe and omit the body.

either succeeds and has no return value or fails with a 400- or 500-series response:

```
Response response = await delete(url);
```

Caution   When making HTTP requests of any type, you should always encode the url before sending. This will help to ensure that the url is valid and can also help with security, especially when taking input from the user. Call Uri.encodeFull like this:

```
String url = Uri.encodeFull('http://us.com/api/
ppl?query=Jo Ki');
```

For simplicity's sake, we're going to omit encoding in the examples. But in the real world, always remember to do this.

Making an HTTP PUT, POST, or PATCH request

PUT, POST, and PATCH are very similar to GET and DELETE. The biggest difference is that PUT, POST, and PATCH all require a body for the request – usually a string with JSON-formatted keys and values:

```
String payload = '{"first":"Kamala", "last":"Khan", "id":374}';
Response response = await post(url, body:payload);
```

This response is unwrapped just as with GET and DELETE requests.

Note   With POST, PUT, and PATCH, we're sending data from the client to the server. It is prudent and sometimes required to also tell the server how we've encoded that data. We'll do that in an HTTP header that we include in the request. Provide a key called "Content-Type" with a value of "application/json". And we'll do that like so:

```
Map<String, String> headers= {'Content-
Type':'application/json'};
Response res = await post(url, headers:headers,
body:payload);
```

While we're on the subject, there are many header variables that you might find helpful like Accept, Accept-Encoding, Authorization, Content-MD5, Cookie, Date, Host, If-Modified-Since, and others. Read about them here: https://en.wikipedia.org/wiki/List_of_HTTP_header_fields#Request_fields.

Making HTTP requests from an API wasn't so bad, now was it? Very quickly we've made our Flutter apps capable of making requests, deserializing the response, and printing that to the debug console. But Flutter is all about displaying that data in cool-looking widgets. So how do we integrate the requests into widgets?

HTTP responses to widgets

There's a handful of ways to wait on the Future to resolve and then display it. We're going to simplify things by showing you only three, the brute force way, FutureBuilder, and StreamBuilder. Brute force is obvious and easy to understand, but I think you'll like FutureBuilder/StreamBuilder because they are cleaner and more elegant.

Brute force – The easy way

You already have all the tools you need to display the data: you understand Futures and you know how to tell the stateful widget to redraw itself with new data – setState(). So it can be as simple as putting a setState() inside the .then() or after the await:

```
String url = 'http://us.com/api/people/12345';
Response response = await get(url);
Map<String, dynamic> responseBody = json.decode(response.body);
String first = responseBody['first'];
String last = responseBody['last'];
String imageUrl = responseBody['profilePictureUrl'];
Widget card = Stack(
  children: <Widget>[
    Image.network(imageUrl,
      height: 300, width: 300, fit: BoxFit.cover),
    Text("$first $last"),
  ],
);
setState(() {
  _cardWidget = card;
});
```

And of course as long as your build method is displaying _cardWidget somewhere, it will be rendered with proper data as soon as the Future is resolved which only happens when the HTTP GET request returns data. Piece of cake! But it isn't the most elegant thing.

FutureBuilder – The clean way

A better solution may be the FutureBuilder widget. If you're ever in a
spot where you have a Future that, when fulfilled, has data that must be
rendered in a Flutter widget look to FutureBuilder. Does this scenario
sound familiar? It should because it is the major reason we have Futures
in Flutter. The simple code example from earlier can be done much more
completely like this with a FutureBuilder:

```
FutureBuilder(
  future: get(url),
  builder: (BuildContext ctx, AsyncSnapshot<dynamic> snapshot) {
    if (snapshot.connectionState != ConnectionState.done) {
      return const CircularProgressIndicator();
    }
    if (snapshot.hasError) {
      return Text('Oh no! Error! ${snapshot.error}');
    }
    if (!snapshot.hasData) {
      return const Text('Nothing to show');
    }
    final Map<String, dynamic> responseBody =
        json.decode(snapshot.data.body);
    final int statusCode = snapshot.data.statusCode;
    if (statusCode > 299) {
      return Text('Server error: $statusCode');
    }
    String first = responseBody['first'];
    String last = responseBody['last'];
    String imageUrl = responseBody['profilePictureUrl'];
```

```
    return Stack(
      children: <Widget>[
        Image.network(imageUrl,
            height: 300, width: 300, fit: BoxFit.cover),
        Text("$first $last"),
      ],
    );
  },
);
```

There's no need for a setState() since the FutureBuilder has access to the Future itself so it knows when and how to redraw itself. In the preceding example, you can see how it is capable of rendering something different for each situation: a ProgressIndicator while we're waiting on the resolution of the Future, an error if something is wrong, a notification if the Future has nothing in it, and of course the widget when the data arrives successfully!

Caution   Always check snapshot.hasData and/or snapshot.hasError before accessing snapshot.data. As of the time of writing,[3] Flutter does not throw if there's an error. Instead, it swallows the error and fails silently.

Also be careful about the HTTP status code which can be found in response.statusCode! If that number is in the 400s or 500s, you've gotten a valid response from the server, but it is a problem and your data will be null.

---

[3]See https://github.com/flutter/flutter/issues/34545 for the proposed changes.

StreamBuilder

What FutureBuilder does with futures, StreamBuilder does with streams. These two classes are nearly identical, having the same format, using the same shape of snapshots, and checking snapshot.hasErrors and snapshot. hasData. But sometimes we're not dealing with a single return of data as with a future, we're dealing with a *stream* of data that may hit us in spurts or waves. When this is the situation, you'll want to use a StreamBuilder instead:

```
StreamBuilder(
  stream: anythingThatReturnsAStream(),
  builder: (BuildContext ctx, AsyncSnapshot<dynamic> snapshot) {
    // Everything below this is pretty much the
    // same as FutureBuilder but the data is a
    // collection of documents, each being a record
    if (snapshot.connectionState != ConnectionState.done) {
      return const CircularProgressIndicator();
    }
    if (snapshot.hasError) {
      return Text('Oh no! Error! ${snapshot.error}');
    }
    if (!snapshot.hasData) {
      return const Text('Nothing yet. Please wait ...');
    }
    return ListView.builder(
      itemCount: snapshot.data.documents.length,
      itemBuilder: (BuildContext context, int i) {
        String first = snapshot.data.documents[i]['first'];
```

```
      String last = snapshot.data.documents[i]['last'];
      String imageUrl = snapshot.data.documents[i]
      ['imageUrl'];
      return Stack(
        children: <Widget>[
          Image.network(imageUrl,
            height: 300, width: 300, fit: BoxFit.cover),
          Text("$first $last"),
        ],
      ),
    },
  );
  );
  },
);
```

Note   Writing code like this, code that wakes up and updates itself based on newly arriving data has a term: *reactive programming*. Reactive programming happens when we make our app aware of its external influences and tell it to react somehow. You may have heard of reactive extensions like rxJava, rxJS, and rx.NET which are libraries with classes and functions made for this style. Well, there is one for Flutter unsurprisingly called rxDart. You can find it at https://github.com/ReactiveX/rxdart.

Strongly typed classes

At this point, you now know how to make HTTP calls against an API, and when you get a response, you know how to unwrap that data and use it. This puts us in a great position to convert that data into a strongly typed class using the typed deserialization pattern.[4]

Note   This is not required in order to make HTTP calls. It is merely a cleaner way of processing the call and pulling it in to a structure that is predictable. HTTP data is by nature unstructured. This is a best practice used by many Flutter developers but is by no means required. So if you don't like it, feel free to skip it.

Typed deserialization happens in three simple steps:

1.   Create the business class.

2.   Write a .fromJSON() method and/or a .fromJSONArray() method.

3.   When reading from HTTP calls, use .fromJSON() to hydrate the object.

Create a business class

Let's say we're reading and writing data for people. We should create a PERSON class:

```
class Person {
  // Constructor only needed b/c the name property is a
  // map of strings and needs to be initialized
```

---

[4]The term "typed deserialization pattern" is one that I coined based on suggestions from the Flutter community. You may not find others using it until it catches on.

```
Person() {
    name = <String, String>{};
}
String documentID;
Map<String, String> name;
String email;
String imageUrl;
}
```

Write a .fromJSON() method

This should be a static method that will return an instance of the business class, Person in this case:

```
class Person {
    // More class code here
    static Person fromJson(String jsonString) {
        final Map<String, dynamic> data = jsonDecode(jsonString);
        return Person()
            ..name = data['name']
            ..email = data['email']
            ..imageUrl = data['imageUrl'];
    }
    // and more class code here maybe
}
```

Note the use of Dart's cascade operators and omission of the *new* operator. Both are best practices also.

Use .fromJSON() to hydrate the object

The word *hydrate* literally means "add water." In this context, the data is the water, and we're creating a new Person object by adding the data to it. You read data from an HTTP service using the .get() method and you pass it into .fromJSON() like this:

```
// Make the HTTP call
final Response res = await get(url);
// Hydrate a Person object from the response body - a JSON
string
Person p = Person.fromJson(res.body);
```

See how clean and straightforward the code is?

I imagine that at this point, you'd like to exercise all of this newfound knowledge. Let's do that with a free API service next.

One big example

A real API service will involve a database with exposed GET, POST, DELETE, PUT, and/or PATCH endpoints which all require some hefty setup on the server. You're going to want to get there eventually, and we'll show you a fantastic permanent solution in the next chapter. But for now, let's make use of a demonstration-only site that costs nothing and is easy to set up so we can build a Flutter app that uses API data.

Let's build a people maintenance CRUD app (Figure 11-1).

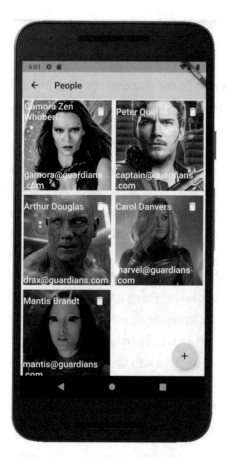

Figure 11-1. *An app to maintain records that reads and writes its data from a RESTful API*

This app will read a list of people from an HTTP web service that conforms to REST principles which means among other things that it supports the HTTP GET, POST, PUT, and DELETE methods we learned earlier. In addition, all records will have a unique ID assigned to them on the server as part of the creation of those records. We'll create the preceding pictured scene to show our list of people. We'll also need another scene with fields to enter the person's name, email address, and the location of a photo.

Sound fun? Well it will be after we get the server set up. Let's start with that.

Setting up

We clearly need a server. So we'll need to stand one up and install and configure a database and a service that receives HTTP requests on port 80 and a bunch of other stuff. Either that or we can use someone else's.

Introducing Pipedream!

Pipedream.com provides cloud-based workflows where even inexperienced developers can easily create complex processes. Their excellent service is also free for reasonable volumes of data and processing. The good folks at Pipedream have created a workflow that exposes a simple RESTful interface, allowing us to read and write data over a public-facing RESTful API with very little effort and at no cost.

You can do all of this anonymously but we recommend that you log into an account so you can revisit the data later. So open `http://pipedream.com` in your browser. Create an account with a password.

Visit this link: `http://bit.ly/pipedream_api`. Hit the big "Fork" button in the upper right. This will create your very own copy that you can own and alter if you need to. At the top of the page you'll see a URL. This is the URL you'll send requests to.

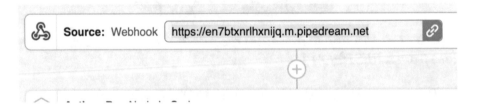

To test it out, get to a command line. Use the curl command to make sure you're set up.

```
$ curl https://en7btxnrlhxnijq.m.pipedream.net
```

If you get a response from the server that says "Success", it is working and you can move on.

Create the Flutter app

Create a new Flutter app using flutter create. Open main.dart and find your MaterialApp widget. Remove the "home" property and add this to it:

```
initialRoute: '/peopleList',
routes: <String, WidgetBuilder>{
  '/peopleList': (BuildContext ctx) => PeopleList(),
  '/peopleUpsert': (BuildContext ctx) => PeopleUpsert(),
},
```

Then make two new StatelessWidgets, one called "PeopleList.dart" and the other called "PeopleUpsert.dart". We'll fill in their details in a minute. But first, it may be a good idea to create a business class to represent a Person object.

Making a strongly typed business class

Since we're working with Persons, it might be a good idea to create a Person class to hold each person. This very optional best practice may help us to avoid bugs serializing and deserializing the server data and give us a centralized place to manage all of our Person-related logic:

```
import 'dart:convert';
class Person {
  // Constructor only needed b/c name is a map of strings
  // and needs to be initialized
  Person() {
    name = <String, String>{};
  }
  // The typed deserialization pattern for a single person
  static Person fromJson(String jsonString) {
```

```dart
    final Map<String, dynamic> data = jsonDecode(jsonString);
    return Person()
      ..id = data['id']
      ..name = data['name']
      ..email = data['email']
      ..imageUrl = data['imageUrl'];
  }
  // The typed deserialization pattern for lists of people
  static List<Person> fromJsonArray(String jsonString) {
    final Iterable<dynamic> data = jsonDecode(jsonString);
    return data.map<Person>((dynamic d) => Person()
      ..id = d['id']
      ..name = {'first':d['first'], 'last':d['last']}
      ..email = d['email']
      ..imageUrl = d['imageUrl']).toList();
  }
  // The actual properties of a person
  int id;
  Map<String, String> name;
  String email;
  String imageUrl;
}
```

PeopleList.dart

We'll eventually read a list of people from the RESTful service and will
want to display their data. The PeopleList widget is responsible for
showing that list of people:

```dart
import 'package:flutter/material.dart';
import 'package:http/http.dart';
import 'Person.dart';
```

```dart
import 'sensitiveConstants.dart';
class PeopleList extends StatefulWidget {
  @override
  _PeopleListState createState() => _PeopleListState();
}
class _PeopleListState extends State<PeopleList> {
  @override
  Widget build(BuildContext context) {
    return Scaffold(
      appBar: AppBar(title: const Text('People'),),
      body: scaffoldBody,
      floatingActionButton: FloatingActionButton(
        // An Add button. When the user taps it, we send
        // them to PeopleUpsert with NO person object.
        child: Icon(Icons.add),
        onPressed: () {
          Navigator.pushNamed(context, '/peopleUpsert');
        },
      ),
    );
  }
  // Note how we pull out details to make the widget more
  // abstract for you. We do the same with personWidget below.
  Widget get scaffoldBody {
    return FutureBuilder<dynamic>(
      future: fetchPeople(), // How we'll get the people
      builder: (BuildContext context, AsyncSnapshot snapshot) {
        if (snapshot.hasError) {
          return Text('Oh no! Error! ${snapshot.error}');
        }
```

```
    if (!snapshot.hasData) {
      return const Text('No people found');
    }
    // Convert the JSON data to an array of Persons
    final List<Person> people =
      Person.fromJsonArray(snapshot.data.body);
    // Convert the list of persons to a list of widgets
    final List<Widget> personTiles = people
        .map<Widget>((Person person) =>
        personWidget(person))
        .toList();
    // Display all the person tiles in a scrollable
    GridView
    return GridView.extent(
      maxCrossAxisExtent: 300,
      children: personTiles,
    );
  },
);
}
// Displaying a single person tile.
Widget personWidget(Person person) {
  // Look in the github source for the details. The
  // important thing is that when the user taps a
  // person tile, we navigate them to PersonUpsert
  // and pass the person object in.
}
}
```

A GET request in Flutter

Look back at getScaffoldBody() method. It has a FutureBuilder. The future property points to a method called fetchPeople() which simply needs to make a GET request to the URL that will respond with a JSON array of Person records:

```
Future<dynamic> fetchPeople() {
  // pipedreamRESTUrl is the URL you made note of before
  final String url =
    '$pipedreamRESTUrl/people/?pipedream_response=1';
  return get(url);
}
```

The GET request is pretty simple once you get the Flutter infrastructure created, huh? Of course when you make this call the first time, nothing will appear since you haven't created any persons yet. That'll come soon enough.

A DELETE request in Flutter

Each person tile has a trashcan IconButton in the upper right. A tap on it calls deletePerson(), receiving the person we want to get rid of. This deletePerson() method should send an HTTP DELETE request, pointing to that person by ID:

```
void deletePerson(Person person) {
  final String url =
    '$pipedreamRESTUrl/people/${person.id}?pipedream_response=1';
  delete(url).then((Response res) {
```

```
      // Call setState() to rerender AFTER the person is gone
      setState(() {
        print('Status code: ${res.statusCode}');
      });
    });
  }
```

Note that after the delete's Future is resolved, we call setState() to force the scene to re-render, thereby refreshing the list of Persons.

PeopleUpsert.dart

We've taken care of reading people and deleting a person in PeopleList. But adding a new person will require a form for the user to enter information. Sharp readers will notice that an identical form is needed for updating existing persons. To adhere to the DRY principle,[5] let's create one form and reuse it for both adding and updating:

```
import 'package:flutter/material.dart';
import 'package:http/http.dart';
import 'Person.dart';
import 'sensitiveConstants.dart';
class PeopleUpsert extends StatefulWidget {
  @override
  _PeopleUpsertState createState() => _PeopleUpsertState();
}
class _PeopleUpsertState extends State<PeopleUpsert> {
  final GlobalKey<FormState> _key = GlobalKey<FormState>();
  Person person;
```

---

[5]https://en.wikipedia.org/wiki/Don%27t_repeat_yourself

```dart
@override
Widget build(BuildContext context) {
  // Get the 'current' person set during navigation. If
  // this person is null, we're adding a new person so
  // we should instantiate one. If this person is not null,
  // then we're updating that person.
  final Person _person =
    ModalRoute.of(context).settings.arguments;
  person = (_person == null) ? Person() : _person;
  return Scaffold(
    appBar: AppBar(
      title: Text(
        (_person == null) ? 'Add a person' : 'Update a
        person',
      ),
    ),
    body: _body,
    floatingActionButton: FloatingActionButton(
      onPressed: () {
        // Commit field data to the form key
        _key.currentState.save();
        // Save the person
        updatePersonToPipedream(person);
        // And go back to where we came from
        Navigator.pop<Person>(context, person);
      },
      child: Icon(Icons.save),
    ),
  );
}
```

```
Widget get _body {
  return Form(
    key: _key,
    child: Container(
      padding: const EdgeInsets.all(20),
      child: Column(
        children: <Widget>[
          TextFormField(
            initialValue: person.name['first'],
            decoration:InputDecoration(labelText:'First name'),
            onSaved: (String val) => person.
            name['first']=val),
          TextFormField(
            initialValue: person.name['last'],
            decoration: InputDecoration(labelText:'Last name'),
            onSaved: (String val) => person.
            name['last']=val),
          TextFormField(
            initialValue: person.email,
            decoration: InputDecoration(labelText:'Email'),
            onSaved: (String val) => person.email=val),
          TextFormField(
            initialValue: person.imageUrl,
            decoration: InputDecoration(labelText:'Image URL'),
            onSaved: (String val) => person.imageUrl=val),
        ],
      ),
    ),
  );
}
}
```

This will create one of pictures in either Figure 11-2 or 11-3.

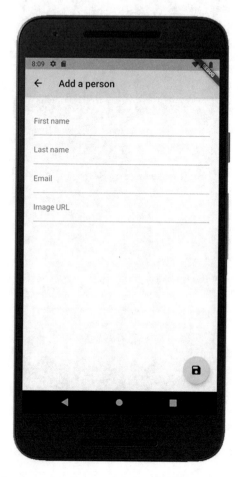

Figure 11-2. *If the user had tapped the "+" button, we're adding*

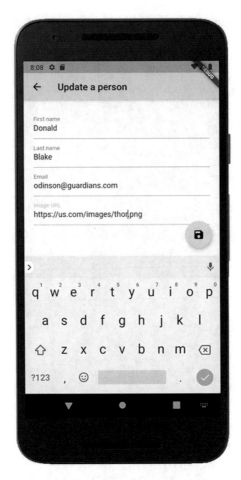

Figure 11-3. *If the user had tapped a person tile, we're updating that person*

A POST and PUT request in Flutter

When the user hits the FAB in the PeopleUpsert scene, they are committing the data they entered and we call updatePersonToPipedream(). If it was an Add operation, we want to make a POST call. If it was an Update operation, we want to make a PUT call:

```
void updatePersonToPipedream(Person person) {
  Future<Response> response;
  final String payload = """
    {
      "first":"${person.name['first']}",
      "last":"${person.name['last']}",
      "imageUrl":"${person.imageUrl}",
      "email":"${person.email}"
    }
    """;
  final Map<String, String> headers = <String, String>{
    'Content-type': 'application/json'
  };
  // If id is null, we're adding. If not, we're updating.
  if (person.id == null) {
    String url =
     '$pipedreamRESTUrl/people/?pipedream_response=1';
    response = post(url, headers: headers, body: payload);
  } else {
    String url =
     '$pipedreamRESTUrl/people/${person.id}?pipedream_
     response=1';
    response = put(url, headers: headers, body: payload);
  }
  response.then((Response res) {
    Navigator.pop(context, Person.fromJson(res.body));
  });
}
```

Conclusion

Not too shabby, huh? We went from knowing almost nothing about reading and writing data via HTTP to a comprehensive example using some fairly advanced techniques like the typed serialization pattern and the FutureBuilder widget.

Unfortunately, though, our examples are using a temporary server-side solution not fit for a production application. Would you be interested in a robust, permanent server-side database that works seamlessly with Flutter on iOS, Android, and the Web? Yes? Well then turn the page and let's learn about Google Firebase!

CHAPTER 12

Using Firebase with Flutter

As an entrepreneur/mentor, I've been pitched a ton of great ideas for business apps. Without exception every one that had any worth has involved a server storing data. So if we care about the real-world use of Flutter, it would be criminal to ignore talking to a production-ready server.

There are no shortage of server solutions out there like AWS from Amazon, Microsoft Azure, IBM Cloud, Oracle Cloud Infrastructure, Alibaba Cloud, and so many others. They're all great. We chose to focus on Firebase, not because it is head and shoulders better than the others but because

1. Firebase and Flutter are both Google products, so there are a few synergies.

2. Firebase is at least as good as, and in some ways better than, the other options.

3. Firebase is (fairly) easy to set up and free for low volumes – perfect for learning and testing.

© Rap Payne 2019
R. Payne, *Beginning App Development with Flutter*,
https://doi.org/10.1007/978-1-4842-5181-2_12

4. Firebase has been getting a ton of attention in the developer community lately. It is becoming the tech that hiring managers and recruiters want to see on your resume.

5. We had to pick one, so why not Firebase? ¯_(ツ)_/¯

If we are going to implement Firebase as a server to use with Flutter, we need to make sure we understand these things:

- Firebase at a very high level

- How to set up a Firebase project

- How to make it work with our eventual iOS and Android apps

- Integrating it in our Flutter app with authorization

- Reading Firestore data into our Flutter app

- Querying data in Flutter

- Changing data in Flutter

- Deleting data in Flutter

So that will be our game plan for this chapter. Let's start with an intro to Firebase itself.

Introducing Firebase

Google Firebase is a set of server-side services and tools. If you use Firebase, you don't need to buy or rent your own server. No applying security patches or updating software. No organizing backups. No configuring of firewalls. No intrusion detection systems. No anti-malware definition maintenance. No paying an ISP to connect to the Internet. Basically, you're trusting Google to handle all of the things you'd do with your own server. Of course a server exists, but you and I don't have access to the OS so we have neither the responsibility nor the ability to maintain it. How freeing is that?

The list of things you cannot do with Firebase is small and not commonly needed. But the list of what you can do is broad and very common. Firebase is made up of over a dozen tools.[1] Let's glance at these three:

- Cloud Firestore – A database with an API to read and write data

- Cloud Functions – Logic that is kicked off by an API call

- Authentication – Single sign-on to allow users to securely log in to your app using their social accounts or a username/password combination

Let's discuss each very briefly and then extend last chapter's example Flutter app to read and write from Firestore.

Cloud Firestore

We want a database that all apps can read from and write to. Firestore provides a NoSQL database with storage and tools to access that data. Being NoSQL it is highly flexible, maybe more flexible than you're comfortable with. If you've worked with MongoDB, Cassandra, or CouchDB, then you know what we're talking about here. The major difference with Firestore is the fact that the database itself and its backend engine are maintained by Google instead of by you and me. All we need to do is access the data.

Firestore exposes API endpoints for the data. After your app identifies itself to Firestore, it can read and write data at those endpoints. Kind of sounds like the RESTful interface we discussed in the last chapter, right?

---

[1]Read about all of them here: https://firebase.google.com/products

Firestore does support an interface that has some features of REST, but it is different enough that I wouldn't categorize it as RESTful. Instead, we use a Dart library that takes care of the heavy lifting of authenticating our app and setting up private communications. We will call methods in that library like Firestore.get('people') or Firestore.set('categories'). This turns out to be much more streamlined once we set it up. (But the setup isn't super simple.)

Cloud Functions

Your app is almost certainly involved in processing data. Some of those algorithms might be very, very complex. But the fact is that your users' devices are probably more than capable of handling those things.

"So why not just process everything in my app? ", you ask. Because if it is on the device, the algorithms could be reverse-engineered by any attacker who downloads your Flutter app. Any secret business processes will be exposed and the logic could be tampered with. Any of your API keys would be stored on your device and could be read. So we would rather not put any sensitive data or processing on the device. Let's put it on the server where it's out of reach.

And what about processes or data that require sharing between two or more apps? You need a server for those things.

You want Cloud Functions for things like

- Consuming a third-party API

- Processing server-side files like spreadsheets

- Extracting, processing, transforming, and loading large data sets

- Running a chatbot or chat application

- Image analysis like face detection or recognizing and extracting text

- Large image processing like blurring offensive images

- Text analysis like intent detection

- Machine learning and AI

- Ordering a product from an ecommerce store like Walmart or Amazon

Cloud Functions are written in JavaScript and run on demand in a Node environment on Google's servers when certain triggers fire like a record is added to Firestore or updated in Firestore, a user logs in, or someone simply makes an Ajax request to a particular URL.

Authentication

Firebase Authentication makes it (relatively) easy to add authentication to your app. Sure, you could add usernames and passwords to your app by brute force, but you'd have to worry about setting up the user tables and writing the authentication logic and hashing the passwords and handling forgotten passwords and all that. With Firebase Authentication, you get all of that functionality along with authentication via Facebook, Github, Twitter, and of course Google itself. Your users can choose to use their own username/password combinations or even do two-factor authentication by SMS message on their mobile devices.

Setting up Firebase itself

All these features and more are available with Firebase. If you want to try out Firebase, it is fun and free and a great learning experience. Besides, it'll give us an opportunity to try out our newly acquired Ajax knowledge in a live read/write environment. We'll let that be our goal over the next pages.

First, you must have an account with Google. If you don't have a Google account, handwrite a letter to Google, place a stamp on it, and snail mail it to "Google Inc., Mountain View, CA 94043."[2]

Go ahead and sign in to your Google Account and visit `http://firebase.google.com` to register an app with Firebase. Follow the prompts. You won't be committing to anything nor pay any money for the basic account.

Over your career, you'll probably be involved in multiple projects, some for learning purposes, some for your side hustles, and maybe even some for your main business. For this reason, Firebase allows users to have multiple projects. We'll create one to work with.

Caution   The following steps are current as of the time of writing, but they can change. Take a look here for the most current steps: `https://firebase.google.com/docs/flutter/setup`.

---

(1) Creating a Firebase project

After logging in to Google, visit console.firebase.google.com and you'll see your console which will eventually feature a list of your projects. Click the button to create a new project. Give the project a name like "Learning Flutter" (Figure 12-1). Figure 12-2 shows the project is good to go.

---

[2]Just kidding. Who doesn't have a Google account?!? Go make one!

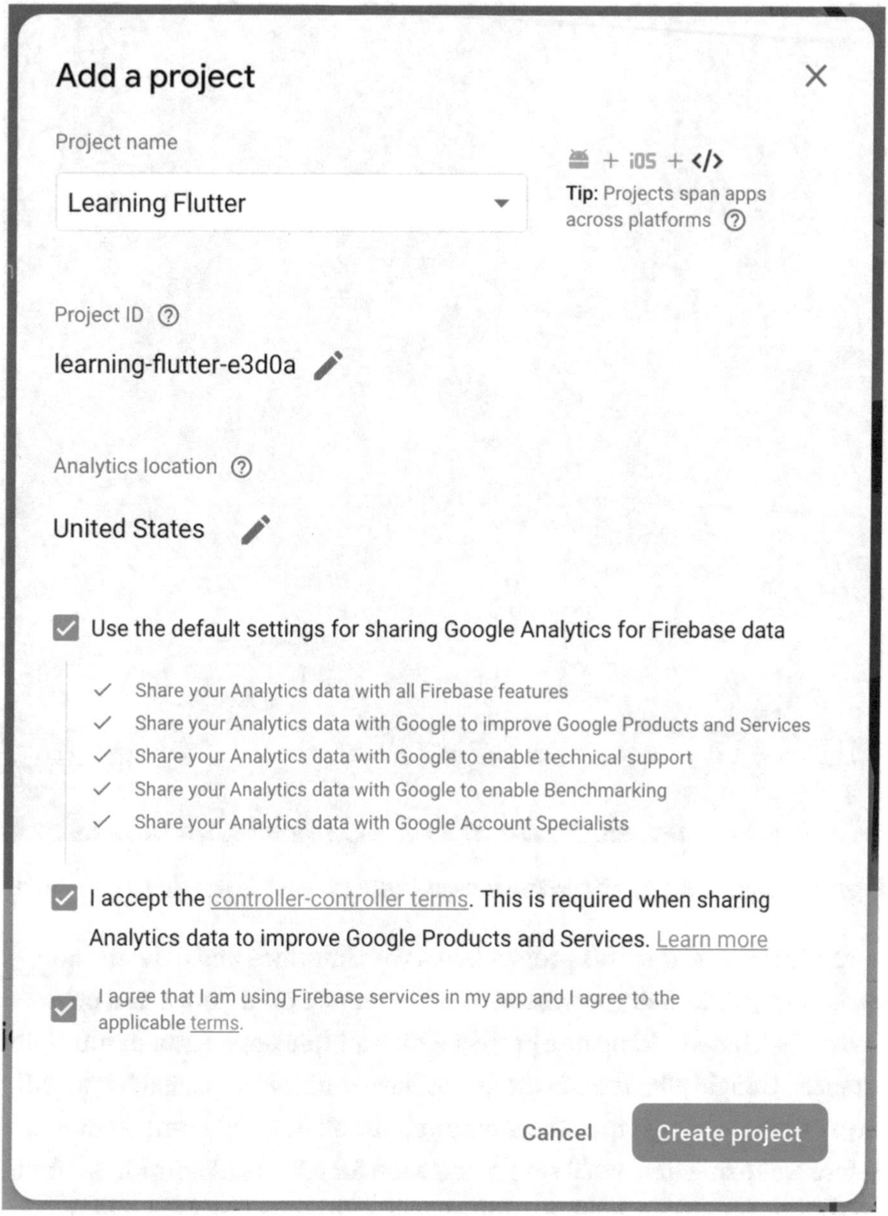

Figure 12-1. *Adding a new project*

Figure 12-2. *The confirmation that your project is ready to go*

Now imagine that this project had a web interface <u>and</u> a database backend <u>and</u> was being accessed by a Flutter app on iPhones and on Androids. This would be one project with multiple apps. As with multiple projects, Google allows each project to have multiple apps. Each app will have its own settings since the environments all have different demands. Before we're finished, we'll set up one each for iOS and Android. But first, we should create our database and at least one collection (aka table).

(2) Creating the database

Go back to your project's dashboard. You'll see a menu choice to develop with a database. Go ahead and choose to create a new database (Figure 12-3).

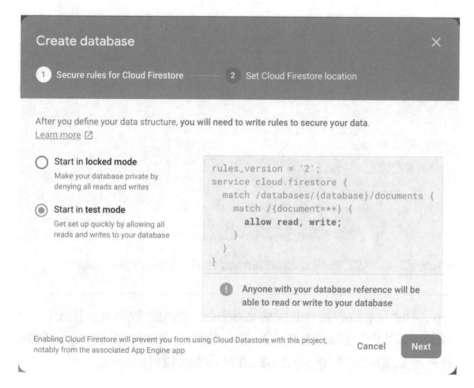

Figure 12-3. *First step in creating a Cloud Firestore database*

Choose to start it out in test mode just so we can easily verify that our code works. You'll want to add rules in a real-world app which you can add at any time. Hit "Next".

This step is asking where the bulk of your users will be physically located (Figure 12-4). It guesses based on your current location, and honestly, any location will work fine. Just take the default and hit "Done". This creates the database.

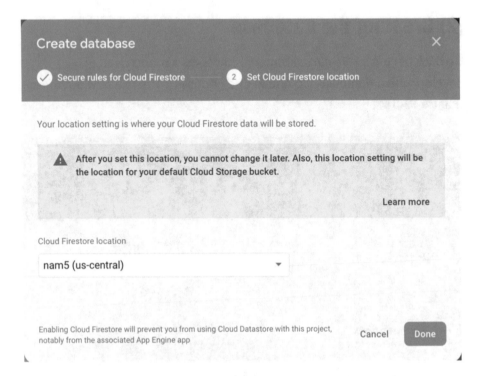

Figure 12-4. *Pick the location closest to the bulk of your users*

Tip   This is a NoSQL database which is different from traditional relational databases like MySQL, SQL Server, Oracle, Informix, and the like. First, the terminology is different (Table 12-1).

Table 12-1. *How you refer to things in different types of DB servers*

Relational databases	NoSQL databases
Tables	Collections
Records/rows	Documents
Columns	Fields

A NoSQL database does have keys and values, but they do not have a fixed structure. In other words, each document in a collection might have different fields than others in that same collection. This is the major difference between traditional databases and NoSQL databases and is the toughest thing to get used to.

Now we'll create a collection. Hit Start Collection and give it an id. Then you'll be able to add one or more documents (Figure 12-5).

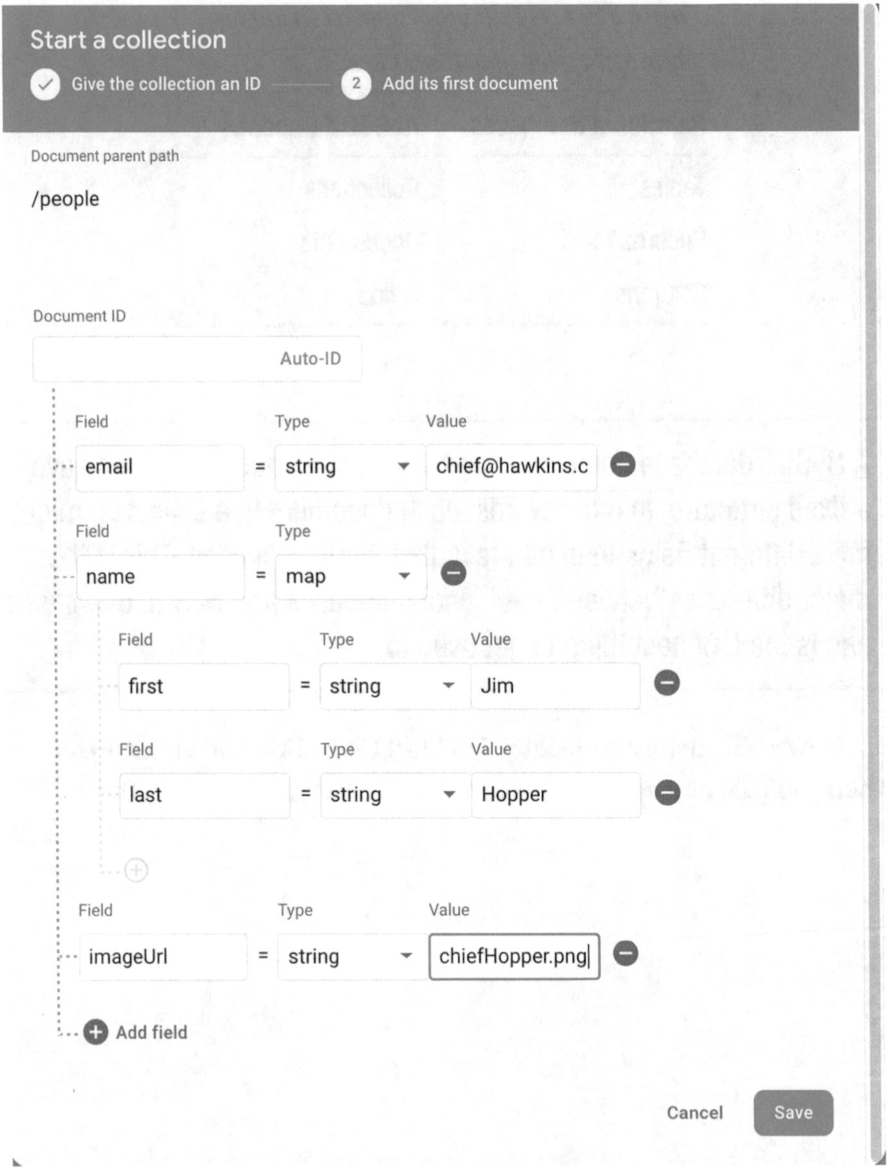

Figure 12-5. *Adding your first document to the collection*

You'll now be able to see your lone document in the Cloud Firestore viewer. From here, you can add documents, delete documents, and alter documents.

It's nice that we can maintain the database right from the Firebase web site, but our goal is obviously to do that from our app. So we must configure our iOS and Android apps to read from Cloud Firestore.

(3) Creating an iOS app

On the overview page for your project, you should see buttons for creating apps in your project (Figure 12-6).

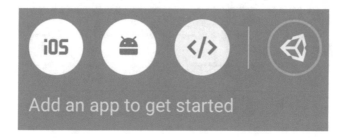

Figure 12-6. *Your options for creating Firestore apps*

Click the iOS button.

Provide a name for the app (Figure 12-7).

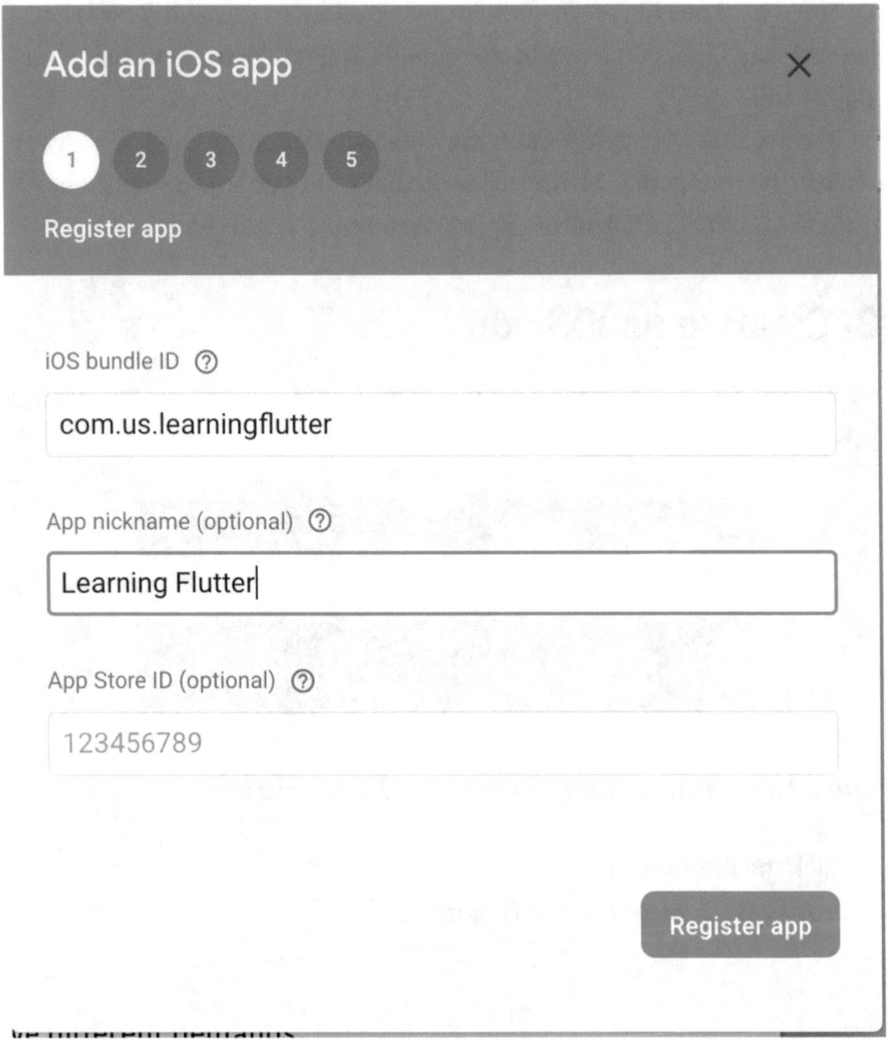

Figure 12-7. *Giving your iOS app an ID and a nickname*

After you register the app, you'll see a view like Figure 12-8.

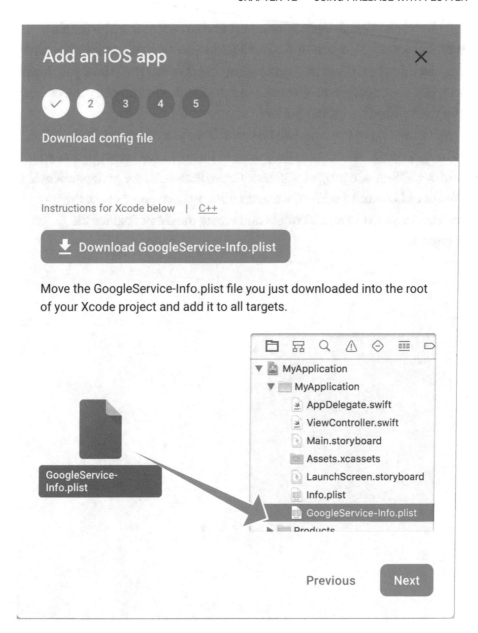

Figure 12-8. *Firestore makes their auto-created config file available for you to download*

Download GoogleService-info.plist and store it in the iOS/Runner/ Runner directory (Figure 12-8). You'll know you're in the right folder when you see Info.plist. Don't be distracted by the diagram they show you. It will look different because they're showing the Xcode version of a project, but you're working in a Flutter project.

Connecting to Firebase will be easier if we use certain tools provided to us by Google. This means they need to be downloaded and installed into our iOS/xcode project. iOS uses CocoaPods to manage dependencies.[3] We should create a Podfile if we don't already have one. Follow the instructions next to add a Podfile and create the .xcworkspace file (Figure 12-9).

---

[3]Like npm/package.json for JavaScript apps, NuGet for .Net, RubyGems for Ruby projects, and so on.

270

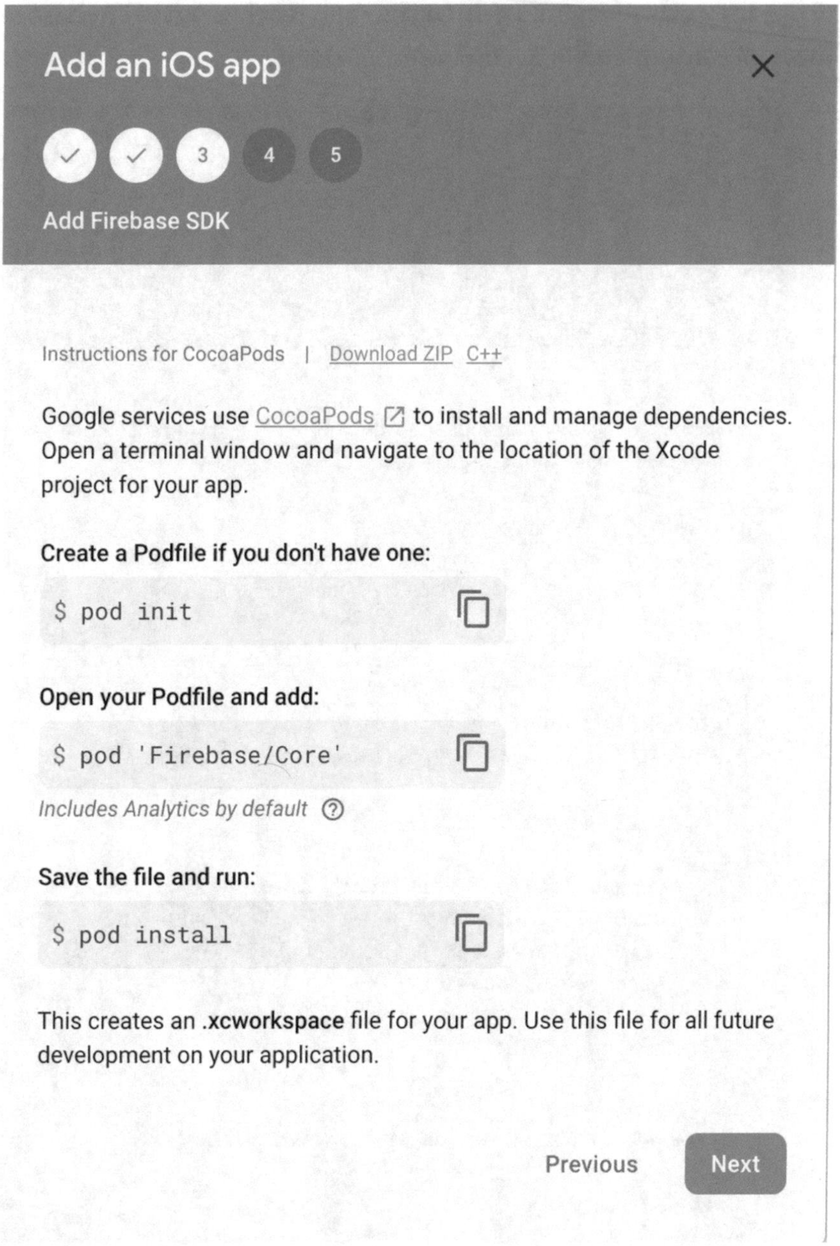

Figure 12-9. *Google provides you the steps to create a Podfile and .xcworkspace*

Copy this code in Figure 12-10 so your app reaches out to Firebase to connect on startup. This is the firebase login logic.

Figure 12-10. *Last step to create your iOS app – add initialization code*

At this point, when your app runs, it knows which Firebase account and project it is associated with. Only an app with this .plist file will be able to connect to your app. Of course, when you compile the app and distribute it to devices through the Apple App Store, they'll all be connecting to this one Firebase account. This is normal and to be expected. Each user who runs it will check in with Firebase. You should see activity in your Firebase console. Firebase is now listening for it and will provide you with analytics data.

Since we're creating a cross-platform app, we should probably also do the same with Android. Remember, they're completely different environments so the steps will be different.

(4) Creating an Android app

Remember where we chose iOS earlier? Now click the Android button shown in Figure 12-11.

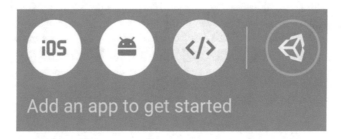

Figure 12-11. *This time choose to add an Android app*

Although the steps are different, the application id or *package name* should be the same. Enter it into the dialog (Figure 12-12).

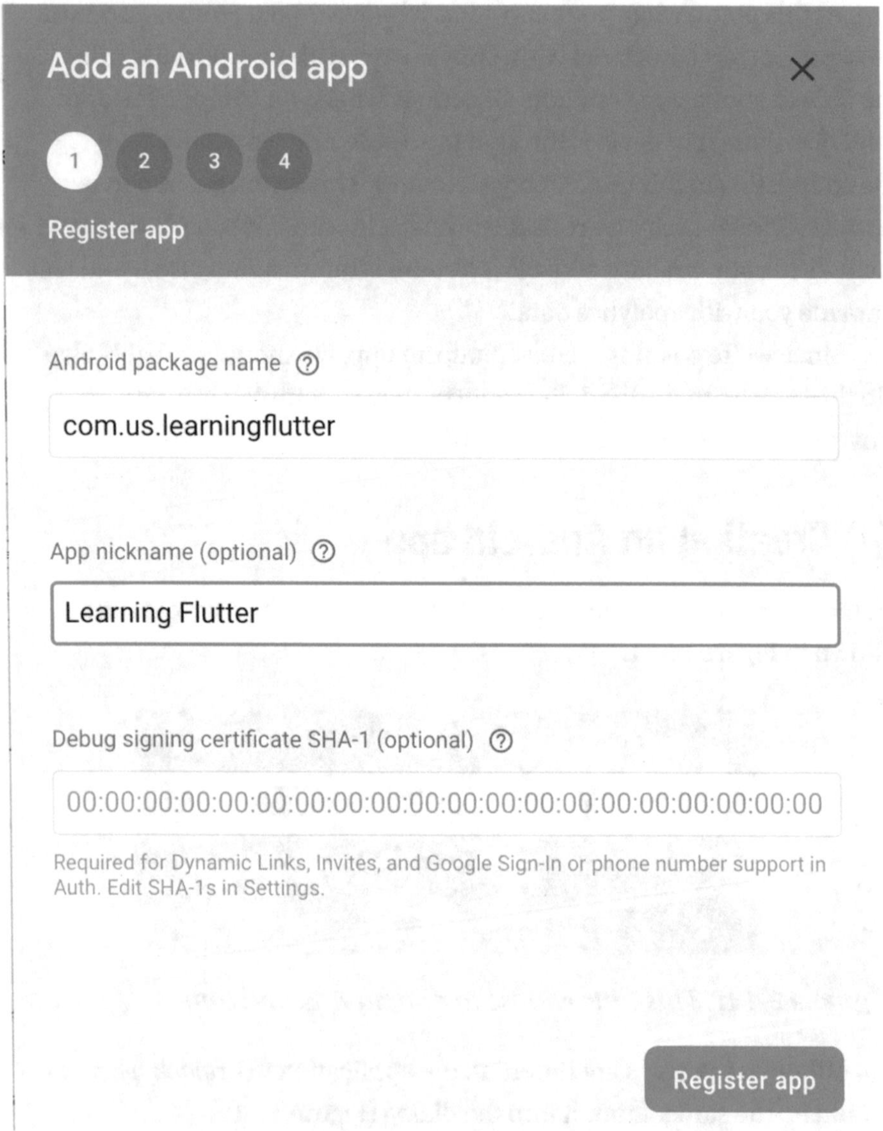

Figure 12-12. *Setting the package name and nickname for Android*

That SHA-1 certificate is optional for most applications. You can leave it blank for now but go back and generate the certificate if you need it for Google Sign-in or phone number authentication.

Install the google-services.json file

Going through the next step, the wizard will create a google-services.json file and will tell you where to save it (Figure 12-13).

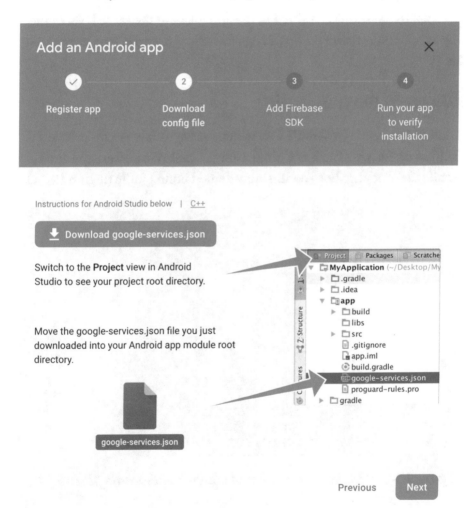

Figure 12-13. *Generate the google-services.json file for Android*

This file has all kinds of important settings in it, especially the project numbers and app ids that will tell your app where to ask for data from Google Firestore. With all of this in a config file, you won't have to hard-code it in your app's source code.

Note that it should be saved in the app folder at the same level as the app-level build-gradle file. Speaking of which, our next step is to edit that file.

Adding to the gradle files

Android projects have Gradle files which manage libraries, much like Podfiles do for iOS. There is a project-level Gradle file and an app-level Gradle file. They are both confusingly named build.gradle (Figure 12-14).

Figure 12-14. *Make sure you know which build.gradle file to edit*

Add this classpath to the dependencies section of the **project-level** build.gradle file, NOT the one under app:

```
buildscript {
    dependencies {
        ( other things may be here already )
        classpath 'com.google.gms:google-services:X.Y.Z'
    }
}
```

Of course, use the latest version number instead of X.Y.Z like earlier. Then add this implementation to the dependencies section of the **app-level** build.gradle file:

```
dependencies {
    ( other things will be here already )
    implementation 'com.google.firebase:firebase-core:X.Y.Z'
}
```

And add this apply plugin to the bottom of the same app-level build. gradle file:

```
apply plugin: 'com.google.gms.google-services'
```

Tell the IDE to sync the gradle files. In Android Studio, you'll see a "Sync now" link. Go ahead and click it.

(5) Adding FlutterFire plugins

Almost there! At this point we have the groundwork laid to use Firebase with our app. We just have to add the Firebase plugins for Flutter and start coding. It turns out that Google provides one common library for Firebase itself and one library plugin for each Firebase product. We'll need the common library plugin and the Cloud Firestore plugin.

The main Firebase plugin is called firebase_core. The plugin for Firestore Cloud Storage is called cloud_firestore. Put these lines in the dependencies section of your pubspec.yaml file and they'll be installed for you:

```
firebase_core: ^X.Y.Z  # main dependency for Firebase Core
cloud_firestore: ^X.Y.Z # dependency for Firebase Cloud Storage
```

Of course if we use other Firestore products, we'll need to add the appropriate plugin, but we won't have to re-do any of the other preceding steps; once for the project is sufficient.

Using Firestore

Yes, that was a lot of setup, but we're finally ready to consume and maintain data from the database. In order to make it easier on you to put these Firestore HTTP calls in context, we'll use the Person examples from the last chapter, replacing the calls to our temporary/test server with calls to Firestore. Refer back to them and to the code from our github repository as you read through the next pages.

At the top of any Flutter dart file that makes Firestore HTTP calls, add an import:

```
import 'package:cloud_firestore/cloud_firestore.dart';
```

This will expose an object called *Firestore* that you can use to get to the database. In fact, Firestore.instance will point to your database as a whole. And Firestore.instance.collection('Foo') will point to the entire Foo collection.

Note   Even though Firestore calls are HTTP calls behind the scenes, there is no need to enter API keys or create setups or post-processing the data or much of the other heavy lifting needed to make normal Ajax calls with Firestore. All of those tasks are abstracted away from you with the inclusion of the libraries which depend on the google-services.json and GoogleService-Info.plist files. As tedious as all that setup was, you can now see the payoff.

To get a collection

As long as you remember that Firestore.instance.collection('Foo') points to the Foo collection, getting that data is easy. You simply call the .snapshots() method to trigger the request. A simple function like this might encapsulate your GET request:

```
Stream<QuerySnapshot> fetchPeople() {
  return Firestore.instance
      .collection('people')
      .limit(100) // Just in case there's a lot of documents
      .snapshots();
}
```

Note that .snapshots() subscribes to a Stream of type QuerySnapshot. And we know from the last chapter that Streams can be displayed and kept up to date with a StreamBuilder widget. This is called reactive programming, remember? Something like this might display that data in a grid:

```
Widget build(BuildContext context) {
 return StreamBuilder<QuerySnapshot>(
    stream: fetchPeople(),
    builder: (BuildContext ctx, AsyncSnapshot<dynamic> snapshot) {
```

```
if (snapshot.hasError) {
  return Text('Oh no! Error! ${snapshot.error}');
}
if (!snapshot.hasData) {
  return const Text('No people found');
}
// The magic! snapshot.data.documents holds your records
final List<Widget> widgets = snapshot.data.documents
  .map<Widget>((DocumentSnapshot p) => Stack(
    children: <Widget>[
      Image.network(p['imageUrl'],
          height: 300, width: 300, fit: BoxFit.cover),
      Text('${p['name']['first']} ${p['name']['last']}',),
    ])).toList();
  return GridView.extent(
    maxCrossAxisExtent: 300,
    children: widgets,
  );
},
);
}
```

Tip   If you want to have a one-time read of the data without subscribing, omit the .snapshot() and it will return a simple array of Maps (aka array of objects). If you do that, you'll want to use a FutureBuilder instead of a StreamBuilder.

To query

Firestore does have a .where() function, but it is very limited compared with a standard SQL where clause. Firestore's .where() will allow you to look for these kinds of things:

```
.where('name.first', isEqualTo: someText)
.where('name.first', isGreaterThanOrEqualTo:someText)
.where('name.first', isLessThanOrEqualTo: someText)
```

And unfortunately that's about it. It does not support any fuzzy logic like wildcards, "contains," or "like." If you need full-text searching, the Firebase team recommends a third-party service like Algolia. See https://firebase.google.com/docs/firestore/solutions/search for more details.

To upsert

The word "upsert" means that if the document exists, it is updated, but if it does not exist, it is added. Firestore does both of these operations with the setData method.

To update an existing document, read it like we did previously and then pass its documentID to setData like so:

```
Firestore.instance
    .collection('people')
    .document(_person.documentID)
    .setData(<String, dynamic>{
  'name': person.name,
  'email': person.email,
  'imageUrl': person.imageUrl,
}).then<void>((dynamic doc) {
  print('Document updated: $doc');
```

```
}).catchError((dynamic error) {
  print('Error! $error');
});
```

If you omit the documentID when calling setData, Firestore assumes you want to add a new record:

```
Firestore.instance
 .collection('people')
 .document()
 .setData(<String, dynamic>{
  'name': person.name,
  'email': person.email,
  'imageUrl': person.imageUrl,
 }).then<void>((dynamic doc) {
  print('Document added: $doc');
 }).catchError((dynamic error) {
  print('Error! $error');
 });
```

Caution   Be careful. It is easy to create duplicates by forgetting the documentID when calling setData().

To delete

Deleting is similarly simple:

```
Firestore.instance
   .collection('people')
   .document(personToDelete.documentID)
   .delete()
```

```
.catchError((dynamic error) {
  print('Error! $error');
});
```

Obviously there is nothing returned from the delete so no need for a .then().

Where to go from here

Let's take a second and look back at the journey we've taken together. Since we began this book ...

- You now understand how Flutter works and is architected

- You can deftly handle the most useful built-in Flutter widgets

- You can create custom widgets, both Stateless and Stateful

- Your Flutter UX can be intuitive through layout widgets

- You can make them look beautiful with styles

- You're able to navigate between scenes in a Flutter app

- You can handle asynchronous activities including reading local data

- You can read and write data through an HTTP/RESTful API

- You can persist data permanently in a robust, scalable server

Wow! That's a ton of stuff! But there are tons more to learn. Heck, even veterans should continue learning. Let me recommend some resources for you to continue to explore and learn.

First, get involved in the Flutter community (of which I'm a member). Start with their Slack channel at `http://flutterStudyGroup.slack.com`. Read their articles at `https://medium.com/flutter-community`. And join us via Zoom on Wednesdays for Hump Day Q & A at `https://tinyurl.com/humpdayqanda` where you can talk live with Flutter devs literally around the globe, ask questions, and even pair program to solve problems. The top Flutter developers in the world hang out there, eager to help you with your Flutter issues.

I also recommend that you subscribe to two free curated emails chock full of Flutter articles, videos, tutorials, and more. Each is delivered freshly baked to your inbox once a week. *Flutter Weekly* has a couple dozen resources per newsletter. Subscribe here: `http://bit.ly/subscribe_to_flutter_weekly`. *Flutter Press Weekly* is smaller each week because it is more selective in the resources shared. You can subscribe to *Flutter Press Weekly* at `http://bit.ly/subscribe_to_flutter_press_weekly`. Reading these regularly will keep your finger on the pulse of the latest developments in Flutter.

Google's Flutter team also has some cool resources. A great place to begin is the Flutter documentation at `https://flutter.dev/docs`. Parts of it are awfully dry to read but is the definitive resource if you're looking up Flutter widgets and APIs. On the other end of the spectrum are their videos, hugely entertaining and easy to digest. I recommend that you subscribe at `http://bit.ly/flutter_youtube_channel`. If you see a "Widget of the Week" video in there, click it immediately! They are one or two minutes at most and will give you a functional understanding of the widget in question faster than anything else. Google is resetting the bar for documentation in their video channel.

I've been overwhelmed with the passion of the Flutter community! If these three mega-resources don't do it for you, there are tons and tons of others out there for the asking. Get involved with your fellow Flutter devs, and if you see me hanging out in one of them, please stop and say hello. Thanks so much for reading!

APPENDIX A

Dart Language Overview

We use the Dart language when writing Flutter, but Dart isn't very popular (yet). Most developers jump right into Flutter with no prior knowledge of the language. In case that's you, we wanted to get you a little assistance.

In this appendix, we're making no attempt to teach you everything about Dart. Our goal here is to get you just enough Dart to be effective as you write Flutter. So this appendix is brief and to the point. We are only dealing with the things that would otherwise have slowed you down while writing Flutter. An example of this is the *rune* data type. Super cool and innovative Dart feature, but rarely used with Flutter so we omitted it. Please try to be tolerant of us if we left out your favorite feature. We didn't forget it. We just decided it wasn't as important as you thought it should be. Please forgive us.

What is Dart?

Dart is a compiled, statically typed, object-oriented, procedural programming language. It has a very mainstream structure much like other OO languages, making it awfully easy to pick up for folks who have experience with Java, C#, C++, or other OO, C-like languages. And it adds some features that developers in those other languages would not expect but are very cool nonetheless and make the language more than elegant.

© Rap Payne 2019
R. Payne, *Beginning App Development with Flutter*,
https://doi.org/10.1007/978-1-4842-5181-2

In light of all that, we've organized this appendix in two sections:

- Expected features – A quick reference (aka a "cheatsheet") of mainstream features, the bare minimum of what you'll need to know for Flutter. You should tear through this section at lightning speed.

- Unexpected features – These are things that might be a surprise to developers who work in traditional OO languages. Since Dart departs from tradition in these areas, we thought it best to explain them briefly – very briefly.

Expected features – Dart Cheatsheet

This quick reference assumes that you're an experienced OO developer and ignores the stuff that would be painfully obvious to you. For a more in-depth and detailed look at Dart, please visit https://dart.dev/guides/language/language-tour.

Data types

```
int x = 10;          // Integers
double y = 2.0;      // IEEE754 floating point numbers
bool z = true;       // Booleans
String s = "hello";  // Strings
dynamic d;           // Dynamic variables can change types
d = x;               // at any time. Use sparingly!
d = y;
d = z;
```

Arrays/lists

```
// Square brackets means a list/array
// In Dart, arrays and lists are the same thing.
List<dynamic> list = [1, "two", 3];
// Optional angle brackets show the type - Dart supports Generics

// How to iterate a list
for (var d in list) {
  print(d);
}
// Another way to iterate a list
list.forEach((d) => print(d));
// Both of these would print "1", then "two", then "3"
```

Conditional expressions

```
// Traditional if/else statement
int x = 10;
if (x < 100) {
  print('Yes');
} else {
  print('No');
}
// Would print "Yes"

// Dart also supports ternaries
String response = (x < 100) ? 'Yes' : 'No';

// If name is set, use it. Otherwise use 'No name given'
String name;
String res = name ?? 'No name given';
```

```
//the "Elvis" operator. If the object is non-null, evaluate
//the property. Prevents null exceptions from throwing.
print(name?.length);
```

Looping

```
// A for loop
for (int i=1 ; i<10 ; i++) {
  print(i);
}
// Would print 1 thru 9

// A while loop
int i=1;
while(i<10) {
  print(i++);
}
// Would print 1 thru 9
```

Classes

```
class Name {
  String first;
  String last;
  String suffix;
}
class Person {
  // Classes have properties
  int id;
```

```
  Name name;     // Another class can be used as a type
  String email;
  String phone;
  // Classes have methods
  void save() {
    // Write to a database somehow.
  }
}
```

Class constructors

```
class Person {
  Name name;
  // Typical constructor
  Person() {
    name = Name();
    name.first = "";
    name.last = "";
  }
}
```

Unexpected things about Dart

The preceding Dart features were unsurprising to any experienced OO developers, but Dart has some pretty cool features that are unique. We'll cover these next, but since they're less familiar, let's take just a sentence or two for each and explain it briefly before giving you a code sample.

Type inference

If I said "x=10.0", what data type would you guess that x is? Double? And how did you know? Because you looked to the right of the equal sign and *inferred* its type based upon the value being assigned to it. Dart can do that too. If you use the keyword var instead of a data type, Dart will infer what type it is and assign that type:

```
var i = 10;          // i is now defined as an int.
i = 12;              // Works, because 12 is an int.
i = "twelve";        // No! "twelve" is a String and not an int.
var str = "ten";     // str is now defined as a String.
str = "a million";   // Yep, works great.
str = 1000000.0;     // Nope! 1000000.0 is a double, not a string.
```

This is often confused with dynamic. Dynamic can hold any data type and can change at runtime. Var is strongly and statically typed.

final and const

final and const are Dart variable modifiers:

```
final int x = 10;
const double y = 2.0;
```

They both mean that once assigned, the value can't change. But const goes a little farther – the value is set at compile time and is therefore embedded in the installation bundle.

final means that the variable can't be reassigned. It does not mean that it can't change. For example, this is allowed:

```
final Employee e = Employee();
e.employer = "The Bluth Company";
```

e <u>changed</u>, but it wasn't <u>reassigned</u> so that's okay. This, however, is not allowed:

```
const Employee e = Employee();
```

const is not allowed at all because this particular class has properties that could potentially change at runtime. final marks a <u>variable</u> as unchangeable, but const marks a <u>value</u> as unchangeable.

So in summary

- dynamic – Can store any data type. The data type can change at any time.

- var – The data type is inferred from the value on the right side of the "=". The data type does not change.

- final – The variable, once set, cannot be reassigned.

- const – The value is set at compile time, not runtime.

Variables are initialized to null

The default data type for most variables is null. The default return value of a function is null:

```
int x;
double y;
bool z;
String s;
dynamic d;
```

All of the preceding data are null since they haven't been assigned a value yet.

String interpolation with $

Interpolation saves devs from writing string concatenations. This ...

```
String fullName = '$first $last, $suffix';
```

... is effectively the same thing as this ...

```
String fullName = first + " " + last + ", " + suffix;
```

When the variable is part of a map or an object, the compiler can get confused, so you should wrap the interpolation in curly braces.

```
String fullName = '${name['first']} ${name['last']}';
```

Multiline strings

You can create multiline strings with three single or double quotes:

```
String introduction = """
Now the story of a wealthy family
who lost everything
And the one son who had no choice
but to keep them all together.
""";
```

Spread operator

The "..." operator will spread out the elements of an array, flattening them. This will be very familiar to JavaScript developers:

```
List fiveTo10 = [ 5, 6, 7, 8, 9, 10, ];
// Spreading the inner array with "...":
List numbers = [ 1, 2, 3, 4, ...fiveTo10, 11, 12];
// numbers now has [1, 2, 3, 4, 5, 6, 7, 8, 9, 10, 11, 12]
```

Map<foo, bar>

Maps are like a hash or dictionary. They're merely an object with a set of key-value pairs. The keys and values can be of any type:

```
// You set the value of a Map with curly braces:
Map<String, dynamic> person = {
  "first": "George",
  "last": "Bluth",
  "dob": DateTime.parse("1972-07-16"),
  "email": "amazingGob@gmail.com",
};
// Angle brackets on a Map set the data types of the keys and
// values. They're not required but are a good practice

// You reference a map member with square brackets:
String introduction = person['first'] + " was born "+
person['dob'].toString();
```

Functions are objects

Just like in JavaScript, functions are first-class objects. They can be passed around like data, returned from a function, passed into a function as a parameter, or set equal to a variable. You can do just about anything with a function that you can do with an object in Java or C#:

```
Function sayHi = (String name) => print('Hello, ' + name);
// You can pass sayHi around like data; it's an object!
Function meToo = sayHi;
meToo("Tobias");
```

Big arrow/Fat arrow

In the preceding example, we also saw the fat arrow syntax. When you have a function that returns a value in one line of code, you can put that returned value on the right side of a "=>" and the argument list on the left side. These are all the same:

```
int triple(int val) {
  return val * 3;
}
Function triple = (int val) {
  return val * 3;
};
Function triple = (int val) => val * 3;
```

The fat arrow is just syntactic sugar, allowing devs to be more expressive with less code.

Named function parameters

Positional parameters are great, but it can be less error-prone (albeit more typing) to have named parameters. Instead of calling a function like this:

```
sendEmail('ceo@bluthcompany.com','Popcorn in the breakroom');
```

You can call it like this:

```
sendEmail(subject:'Popcorn in the breakroom',
  toAddress:'ceo@bluthcompany.com');
```

Now the order of parameters is unimportant. Here is how you'd write the function to use named parameters. Note the curly braces:

```
void sendEmail({String toAddress, String subject}) {
  // send the email here
}
```

Named parameters also work great with class constructors where they are very commonly used in Flutter:

```
class Person {
  Name name;
  // Named parameters
  Person({String firstName, String lastName}) {
    name = Name()..first=firstName..last=lastName;
  }
}
```

Omitting "new" and "this."

In Dart, it is possible – and encouraged – to avoid the use of the *new* keyword when instantiating a class:

```
// No. Avoid.
Person p = new Person();
// Yes
Person p = Person();
```

In the same way, inside of a class, the use of "this." to refer to members of the class is not only unneeded because it is assumed, but it is also discouraged. The code is shorter and cleaner:

```
class Name {
  String first;
  String last;
  String suffix;
  String getFullName() {
    // No. Avoid "this.":
    String full=this.first+" "+this.last+", "+this.suffix;
```

```
  // Better.
  String full=first+" "+last+", "+suffix;
  return full;
 }
}
```

Class constructor parameter shorthand

Merely a shorter way of writing your Dart classes which receive
parameters. When you write the constructor to receive "this.something"
and have a class-scoped property with the same name, the compiler writes
the assignments so you don't have to:

```
class Person {
  String email;
  String phone;
  // The parameters are assigned to properties automatically
  // because the parameters say "this."
  Person(this.email, this.phone) {}
}
```

The preceding code is equivalent to

```
class Person {
  String email;
  String phone;
  Person(String email, String phone) {
    this.email = email;
    this.phone = phone;
  }
}
```

Private class members

Dart does not use class visibility modifiers such as public, private, protected, package, or friend like other OO languages. All members are public by default. To make a class member private, put an underscore in front of the name:

```dart
class Person {
  int id;
  String email;
  String phone;
  String _password;

  set password(String value) {
    _password = value;
  }
  String get hashedPassword {
    return sha512.convert(utf8.encode(_password)).toString();
  }
}
```

In that example, id, email, and phone are public. _password is private because the first character in the name is "_", the underscore character.

Mixins

Mixins are baskets of properties and methods that can be added to any class. They look like classes but cannot be instantiated:

```dart
mixin Employment {
  String employer;
  String businessPhone;
```

```
void callBoss() {
  print('Calling my boss');
  }
}
```

A mixin is added to a class when it uses the "with" keyword:

```
class Employee extends Person with Employment {
  String position;
}
```

This Employee class now has employer and businessPhone properties and a callBoss() method:

```
Employee e = Employee();
e.employer = "The Bluth Company";
e.callBoss();          // An employee can call its boss.
```

Dart, like Java and C#, only supports single inheritance. A class can only extend one thing. But mixin members are added to a class so any class can implement multiple mixins and a mixin can be used in multiple other classes.

The cascade operator (..)

When you see two dots, it means "return this class, but before you do, do something with a property or method." We might do this

```
Person p = Person()..id=100..email='gob@bluth.com'..save();
```

which would be a more concise way of writing

```
Person p = Person();
p.id=100;
p.email='gob@bluth.com';
p.save();
```

No overloading

Dart does not support overloading methods. This includes constructors.

Named constructors

Since we can't have overloaded constructors, Dart supports a different way
of doing essentially the same thing. They're called named constructors and
they happen when you write a typical constructor, but you tack on a dot
and another name:

```dart
class Person {
  // Typical constructor
  Person() {
    name = Name()..first=""..last="";
  }
  // A named constructor
  Person.withName({String firstName, String lastName}) {
    name = Name()
      ..first = firstName
      ..last = lastName;
  }
  // Another named constructor
  Person.byId(int id) {
    // Maybe go fetch from a service by the provided id
  }
}
```

And to use these named constructors, do this:

```
Person p = Person();
// p would be a person with a blank first and last name

Person p1 = Person.withName(firstName:"Lindsay",lastName:"Fünke");
// p1 has a first name of "Lindsay" and a last name of "Funke"

Person p3 = Person.byId(100);
// p3 would be fetched based on the id of 100
```

Index

A

AlertDialog, 154
Android
      emulator, 14, 15
Android Studio, 11
Android Virtual Device (AVD)
      manager, 14, 15
Anti-RaisedButton, 81
API call, 228
API requests, 228, 229
AppBar widget, 103, 104
async, 215
await, 214

B

BLoC, 200, 201
Boolean value
      property, 60
BoxConstraints, 106
BoxFit options, 52
BoxFit.scaleDown, 51
Box model, 124
BoxShape, 173
build.gradle file, 276
Button widgets, 78

C

Cascade operator (..), 300
Class visibility modifiers, 299
Cloud firestore, 257, 258
Cloud functions, 258, 259
ColorCircle, 197
ColorMixer, 195
ColorValueChanger, 197
Column widget, 111
Compile-to-native cross-platform
      frameworks, 7
Componentization, 34
Container
    alignment property, 126, 127
    <div>, 125
    properties, 125
    size, 128–130
crossAxisAlignment, 115, 117
Cross-platform development
      categories, 6
CRUD app, API service, 241
    DELETE request, 247
    Flutter app, creation, 243
    GET request, 247
    PeopleList widget, 244–246
    PeopleUpsert.dart, 248–252

© Rap Payne 2019
R. Payne, *Beginning App Development with Flutter*,
https://doi.org/10.1007/978-1-4842-5181-2

X, Y, Z

Printed in the United States
By Bookmasters